SECRETS OF SELF-MASTERY

SECRETS OF SELF-MASTERY

AN INSPIRATIONAL GUIDE
TO THE MASTERY OF LIFE

Lowell Russell Ditzen, D.D., LL.D.

PASTOR
THE REFORMED CHURCH OF BRONXVILLE
NEW YORK

HENRY HOLT AND COMPANY, NEW YORK

Library of Congress Catalog Card Number: 58-7639

First Edition

Grateful acknowledgment is made to the following publishers
and authors for granting permission to use excerpts in this volume.

"Quiet Is What We Need" by Christopher Morley, *Atlantic
Monthly,* January, 1947

"Man-Test" in THE SHOES OF HAPPINESS AND OTHER
POEMS by Edwin Markham, Copyright 1915 by Edwin
Markham, Doubleday and Company, Inc.

"Deep Is the Hunger" by Howard Thurman, published by
Harper and Brothers

"Two Gods" by Sam Walter Foss in MASTERPIECES OF
RELIGIOUS VERSE, Harper and Brothers, 1948

RENASCENCE AND OTHER POEMS, Harper and Brothers,
Copyright c 1912, 1940 by Edna St. Vincent Millay

EACH IN HIS OWN TONGUE by H. W. Carruth, G. P.
Putnam's Sons, Copyright 1908, renewed 1936 by Katherine
M. Carruth

81864-0318

To
Virginia Stuart Ditzen
Stuart and Deborah

This book by a wise and kindly man is a volume of unusual helpfulness. It goes deeply into the basic problems of modern individuals and comes up with answers that really answer. Pleasant, literary quality is blended with satisfying practicality.

The book is directed to human need as all of us face it daily. Dr. Ditzen's thoroughgoing scholarship and profound understanding are communicated in a charming and highly readable style.

SECRETS OF SELF-MASTERY can mean much to the reader personally and is also an excellent tool for helping other people.

NORMAN VINCENT PEALE
February, 1958

CONTENTS

I

KEEPING WATER
IN THE
DEEP WELLS

. . . as he thinketh in his heart so is he.

Proverbs 23:7

He that hath no rule over his own spirit is like a city that is broken down, and without walls.

Proverbs 25:28

Over the time thou hast no power; to redeem a world sunk in dishonesty has not been given thee; solely over one man therein thou has a quite absolute, uncontrollable power; him redeem.

Carlyle

When Alexander had subdued the world, and wept that none were left to dispute his arms, his tears were an involuntary tribute to a monarchy that he knew not,—man's empire over himself.

Jane Porter

No man is free who cannot command himself.

Pythagoras

Pursue, keep up with, circle round and round your life, as a dog does his master's chaise. Know your own bone; gnaw at it, bury it, unearth it, and gnaw it still.

Thoreau

SOME MONTHS AGO I traveled for several days along the dusty roads of southern India with three educated and intelligent Indians. They were alive to the tensions of the world and eager to discuss and debate, and we spent much time talking about the differences and frictions between the Orient and the Occident. One afternoon, as we were dodging the perennial ox carts and animals on the road, one of the three told of a European engineer who came to India to give technical supervision to a vital industrial project. He did his work well. But his influence was greatly diminished in Indian eyes when on one occasion he lost his temper. Another of the Indians broke in: "You see, self-control and discipline are among our highest virtues." The third added, "Our sages put it this way: 'He who can master himself can control the world.'"

Those words which have often returned to me, speak pertinently to all men of the urgent needs in our modern Western life. The distilled wisdom of the meditative Indian thinker has its counterpart in many races and generations. Plato said for his time and for all time, "For the man who makes everything that leads to happiness, or near to it, to depend upon himself, and not upon other men, . . . such a one . . . has adopted the very best plan for living happily." He, with other ancient Greek and Roman thinkers, was indicating that the happiness to be gained from life comes from within. To ignore the right inward adjustments of your needs and desires and outlooks is to make well-being impossible.

The Bible repeats this counsel many times. "He that ruleth his own spirit is better than he that taketh a city," is a theme played with many variations in the holy book of the Jew and the Christian.

Louis XIV, King of France, in one of the longest reigns in European history, from 1643 to 1715, faced unending sovereign problems. Although the Peace of Westphalia was signed in 1648 and the Peace of the Pyrénées in 1659, there began in 1667 a long series of wars that lasted with little intermission to the end of his reign. France experienced successes and defeats on the field. Some domestic forward movements were made, but there were setbacks too. Strong achievements in the political sphere marked his reign, but there also were grave mistakes that were injurious to France. Louis XIV was expressing the wisdom learned by hard experience when he stated, "There is little that can withstand a man who can conquer himself."

Louis XIV was saying what the Indian sages had said long before: "He who can master himself can control the world." Therein lies the key to the solution of many of our modern dilemmas, the answer to many of our personal and corporate problems, to some of our most poignant needs. The truth is affirmed that *there can't be mastery of life on any frontier until individuals grow first in the art of mastering themselves.*

Each of our national holidays racks up another high score of deaths on the highways. How many, I wonder, of the causes listed in reports written by officers—if all the facts were known—might not really be: "irritation—that stepped on the accelerator too fast"; or "fear—that jammed on the brakes too hurriedly"; or "the devil-may-care attitude that threw discretion to the winds and gambled with tons of steel rushing at seventy miles an hour." Couldn't all of these be more accurately labeled "lack of self-mastery"? How can there be control on the highways until there are individuals who know how to control themselves?

One in three of our marriages ends in separation. I am sure that not one in a million starts out from the station labeled "Wedded Life," intending to end up at the terminus called "Divorce." Why then is it so?

The reasons are as legion as the individual situations. But those who serve as counselors attest that all too often the discipline that could have restrained the sharp word or the selfish attitude or the cruel act was absent. The control that provides patience, the wisdom that comes from standing by commitments and responsibilities, were never achieved.

A successful marriage, a secure home, requires individuals who face up to their partnership—not according to some intricate blueprint for wedded life, not by one mate's determination to control and dominate the other. There must be first of all a sincere effort to master themselves.

Let us look at our personal histories. Won't most of us admit that our most tragic mistakes, our deepest remorse, our most wretched unhappiness, were not caused by someone else's follies? The real cause was some lack within ourselves. And is it not true that our finest achievements, our deepest pleasures, which stand noble and clearly etched in memory, were created by our own efforts, by self-mastery? Each of us has known the warm glow that is our reward for having made a sure step forward in mastering ourselves.

The spokes in the wheel of self-mastery are many and complex. In this volume we will think about them together. The analogy of a wheel is a good one. The wheel eases the load; it helps move the weight. If properly rounded and supported by a firm hub and strong, well-placed spokes, it carries the load in purposeful fashion.

The first thing for us to put in place is the hub of the

wheel. All else is related to and dependent on it. The hub
can be defined simply: The real mastery of life comes with
growth in Godliness. It can be said another way: We grow
in self-mastery to that degree that there enters into our thinking and feeling the creative and perfect spirit which has made
this creation for order, for justice, for truth, for beauty, for
love, and for peace. It can be expressed simply, but it is the
most powerful and profound thought in all creation.

In a later chapter of this book there will be a fuller consideration of the concept of God. But I think it is important
to emphasize now that we will hold to no restrictive theo-
logical definition of the term "God." We can find revelations
of that creative force called God in all religions; and there
are glimpses of God in everything that is good and true and
beautiful.

Shelley was expelled from Oxford University on the charge
of atheism. In his own words he made the profession that he
was devoted to that "beauty which penetrates and clasps and
fills the world, scarce visible for extreme loveliness." We
would not exclude Shelley; we would say that indeed he had
a devotion to the spirit that we are calling God.

There cannot be a limited definition of God. The finite
cannot completely define the infinite. That which is limited,
such as the mind of man, cannot circumscribe the limitless.
After observing how the same chameleon appeared as red in
color to one man and blue to another, Ramakrishna observed, "The devotee who has seen God in one aspect knows
Him in that aspect only. But he who has seen Him in mani-
fold aspects is alone in a position to say: 'all these different
forms are of one God . . .' " The Christian faith affirms that
Jesus reveals more of God than man had seen before. But
Jesus Himself did not limit the concept of God to what can
be found in Him. He affirmed, "The Father is greater than
I."

Henry Sloan Coffin has used an analogy I find helpful. He

tells how he and fellow campers were seeking a water supply for a cabin in the mountains. On a hillside there were evidences of water. But those who examined the area had various opinions. One, seeing signs of dampness, was of the opinion that there was not a spring there. It was only slight drainage of the hillside. Another noted that not in one but in several places there were tiny trickles of water, which seemed to substantiate the theory that there really wasn't any one dependable stream. Another, looking at the site, felt that while there surely was some water located below the surface, there probably wasn't enough to supply the needs of the camping headquarters to be established below.

Excavation, however, showed that the several damp areas, made by tiny streamlets, converged into one fine spring, producing an abundant flow. After the spring had been walled up into a well hole, it provided, on the hottest days of August, all the water needs for the campers and their families vacationing down in the valley.

This analogy casts light on one facet of understanding the great gem called God. While there are many manifestations, there is one ultimate source of refreshment. Often it is indifferently passed by, as was the unseen spring beneath the topsoil on the mountainside. But still it is there and, properly cleared and channeled, can be the source of life to those who live nearby.

George Matheson summed up one aspect of the thought when he wrote:

> Make me a captive Lord,
> And then I shall be free;
>
> * * * *
>
> I sink in life's alarms,
> When by myself I stand;
> Imprison me within Thine arms
> And strong shall be my hand.

By whatever road man comes to God, it is there he finds his replenishment, his life.

As we think about self-mastery, let us not identify it with the notion of a Spartan discipline that stands rigid and inflexible; do not visualize that stern form of repression that digs in when it should bend before the storms of fate. There are, of course, times when it is necessary to hold the doors fast against cringing fear and cowardice. There are occasions when all of us must be able to say:

> In the fell clutch of circumstance
> I have not winced nor cried aloud
> Under the bludgeoning of chance
> My head is bloody but unbowed.

But not all the time. A firm hand and an iron arm are only a part of the secret.

What we are seeking is a broader, deeper association that not only strengthens each individual for the hurricane tragedies of life, but prepares him for the day-by-day business of living. Man must be competent to meet the tiny irritations, the dull, picayune decisions. The continuous exercise of sheer will power places an unbearable strain on an individual, whose taut nerves are one day bound to snap. Who wants to hide behind barred gates all the time, smothering passions, repressing concerns, fearing the acts of fate? Don't we prefer to keep the doors open, knowing that we can handle whatever comes, safe in the confidence that we are not slaves but masters?

Each of us can sweep our soul clean of the devils. In their place will live a stronger spirit, illuminating that center of our being, which will drive the devils farther and farther into the darkness.

In Dostoevski's great book, *Crime and Punishment*, a young student, Raskolnikov, falls under the domination of

a terrifying idea: "I am the final judge of my own thoughts
and deeds . . . who dares to tell me what I am allowed and
not allowed to do?" He then murders two women and con-
dones his vicious acts by saying, "Am I not free to kill a
loathesome, disgusting woman, if I find it convenient to do
so?"

He chances to meet a girl named Sonia, who has been
forced into prostitution to make money that her family might
eat. In spite of her slavery, Sonia has remained pure in spirit
and devout in her faith. There is an unforgettable scene, in
a shabby room, as Sonia reads from the Bible to Raskolnikov
the story of Lazarus being raised from the dead. Through
the simple trust of that girl, reading the words of an ancient
miracle, another miracle is wrought. The devil born of Raskolnikov's violent idea is driven out as God, the spirit of
justice, of compassion, enters his troubled soul and he learns
the wisdom of Proverbs: ". . . cease from thine own wisdom."

Moved by remorse and repentance, Raskolnikov gives himself to the law and goes into penal servitude in Siberia. But
though the man is chained, there is the feeling that he goes
to a slave's drudgery a more masterful man than he ever was
in his so-called liberty. He illustrates the truth, "Make me a
captive Lord, And then I shall be free."

The final mastery of life is determined by who or what is
master of ourselves. If we add to our deepest sensibilities the
universal compassion, kindness, justice, wisdom, and harmony that are imbedded in the core of creation, we are, in
some sense, mastered. But we are masterful.

We do not achieve this goal without thought and concern. The four walls of an empty apartment, transformed
into a home of order and beauty, took someone's vision and
effort. It is so too with the formation of the hub of our self-
mastery. The "God-sense" takes time and effort.

One way we achieve it is by constantly exposing our mind

to exalted thought and ennobling emotion. From the psychological standpoint it might be termed "educating the subconscious."

We become what we think! Our spiritual health is the result of our spiritual diet. We say that "we act according to our lights." But what "light" we have is the result of the experiences we have had, the ideas we have permitted to grip us, the ideal to which we have habitually looked, the kind of people with whom we have associated.

Haven't you found at night in those times between wakefulness and sleep, or when the subconscious comes to the borderline of consciousness, that light is sometimes shed on problems that are of primary concern? Occasionally, at those times, answers come or solutions are provided that seemed elusive in the conscious, day-to-day activity.

It is clear that the capacity to find an answer, discover a solution, is achieved by having stored the reservoirs of both the conscious and the deeper-than-conscious with high thought and deep feeling.

One man I know who has had an amazing facility for solving problems has told me that his secret is the Bible. Since boyhood he has read a chapter each day and also some inspiring literature. He has shunned people who would waste his time and has sought out those who have achieved.

When there is a difficulty he cannot quickly manage in the push of the day's activity, he postpones it for "a spiritual fishing expedition." That is a time when he goes into a room alone, relaxes, and seeks to let his conscious thought be filled with perfect love and compassion, goodness and truth. He lets in "as much of what God is as possible into my awareness." Only then does he look at his problem. All who know that man will tell you of the soundness, and often the uncanny rightness, of his judgments. We in similar fashion will achieve a growing mastery as we nourish our minds with quiet meditation and inspiring truth. We can daily educate the subconscious to provide light for our dark times.

I've never been to Oberammergau. But the vivid and glowing reports of that Alpine valley have carried me in imagination to that place, where the simple natives for generations have yearly produced a moving Passion play. From childhood the people of Oberammergau prepare for the role they will play in that portentous drama depicting the life and death of Jesus. I have been told that the visitor to Oberammergau is struck not only by the acting on the stage but by the feeling that the people seem to live their parts each hour of the day. Living all their lives with the picture of the ideal, not only do they master the play, but it begins to master them, until, in their shops and homes, they show something of the dignity, of Peter and James and John. They reflect something of the aura of the Divine Carpenter Himself.

You may legitimately say that this tense life of ours is in wide contrast to the uncomplicated life in that hamlet nestled in the Bavarian Alps. I will not dispute that. But our need for self-mastery is, therefore, greater still. Individuals today face decisions that affect the lives of many, decisions that call for vision and right and deep wisdom. There is a need for commanding, masterful attitudes in our homes, in our communities, in our national life—attitudes that can heal frictions and bring together opposing points of view. God knows that we need to speak words we shall not have to recant or regret. We need a stability that will keep us on an even keel.

The surest way to get it is to practice the art whose creed is, "I will let more and more of The Perfect Spirit into the abode of my imperfections."

To the people of my parish I recently made a suggestion that has as much value as almost all else in my seven years of preaching and teaching. I asked that every one of us begin each day with God. It is one of the most powerful suggestions I can give to you.

Begin a regular regime of opening and closing each day with eternity, with the "foreverness" of order and holiness and good will. No matter where you are or what you are doing—driving to work, jostling along on the subway, returning from taking the children to school, or doing the breakfast dishes—say, in your own words, "Let there be in me this day something of the silence and goodness and righteousness and love that is at the heart of eternity."

This is the beginning and the end of the secret of growing self-mastery:

> We will not master be
> Until we Master find.

II

USING QUIET

FOR

SELF-MASTERY

In returning and rest shall ye be saved; in quietness and in confidence shall be your strength.

Isaiah 30:15

Be it mine to draw from wisdom's fount, pure as it flows, that calm of soul which virtue only knows.

Aeschylus

Silence is the element in which great things fashion themselves together; that at length they may emerge, full-formed and majestic, into the daylight of Life, which they are thenceforth to rule.

Carlyle

Coolness and absence of heat and haste, indicate fine qualities. A gentleman makes no noise, a lady is serene.

Standing on the bare ground—my head bathed by the blithe air, and uplifted into infinite space—all mean egotism vanishes . . . The currents of the universal being circulate through me.

Emerson

I have often said that all the misfortunes of men spring from their not knowing how to live quietly at home in their own rooms.

Pascal

S OME TIME AGO, at the season of the year when goldenrod dominates the meadows and bright red leaves challenge the solemn advance of winter, I received a letter from an old friend. "It seems almost unbelievable," he wrote, "that a few weeks ago I was paddling a canoe at night on a sequestered woodland lake. I was completely alone. A full moon was shining. I had an experience then," he went on to say, "that must have been something like that of Admiral Byrd when he was alone in the Antarctic for so many months. You may recall how he spoke of feeling himself a part of the mystic harmony of all creation."

He continued, "I was beginning to find something of myself. There were responsivenesses that I didn't know I had. But that's all now far away and gone as I get pounded hour in and hour out by the pressures of my business and my demanding family at home."

There was a wistfulness in that letter that haunts me still in recalling it. It was clear that something very important was being crowded out—something that only quiet and solitude were beginning to create or restore in that man.

Christopher Morley was telling of his need and that of us all who live in this clamorous time when he wrote:

> Quiet is what we need. By telephone,
> The press, the mail, the doorbell, radio
> AP or NAM or CIO,
> We're micro-organized and overgrown

With everybody's business but our own;
Pipe it down, chain talkers. Muffle and slow
The rapid pulse. I wonder if you know
How good it feels, sometimes to be alone?

Incessantly loquacious generation,
Let yeah and nyah be your communication.
Before the world comes open at the seams
Invest some private enterprise in dreams.
In unimpassioned silence we might find
(If ever) what the Author Had in Mind.

Some of the most important steps we take on the road to
self-mastery are steps that must be taken alone, in the depths
of our quietude. Like the silent roots of a tree that go deep
into the earth and grapple and move the stones they encircle,
so it is the right use of quietness that grow the roots of confidence into our personalities.

Isaiah, the prophet, a man of steel conviction, a man who
dealt head-on with perplexing problems in his own generation, was also saying this, not merely to his day but to ours:
"In returning and rest shall ye be saved; in quietness and in
confidence shall be your strength."

You and I probably would like to say to Isaiah, "You're
hitting the nail on the head for us. We need strength. We
need confidence for our tasks and our dilemmas. We'd like to
know your secret. As we read your biography, Isaiah, we
know what a stalwart prophet you were. You faced life
squarely. We'd like to have what you had. Didn't you get
your strength from those direct and unflinching charges into
the sociological and political issues of your day?"

"On, no, no," replies Isaiah, "that isn't the way at all. It's
a returning—a returning to the solemnity, the mysteries, the
grandeur whence your spirit came. I know from experience
that this is the secret. Elijah, a prophet long before me, found
it out. He said that you don't discover it in outward noise
and conflict. You find it by listening to the still, small voice.

And the condition for hearing it is solitude and quiet. You must make for yourself a time of tranquillity. You have to keep a core of calmness that nothing on the outside can touch. You see, the strength of which I am speaking, the strength that means victory in noisy battles, comes first of all from some silent time when you've had the chance to cultivate your inner confidence alone."

Look at some aspects of the controlled spirit and see how they have to be tapped to some roots of quiet.

This is the matter of your own individuality. Each of us, every human being in the world, is distinct. That raw stuff of our unique selfhood is our most precious possession. But how easily it gets buffeted and crushed by what other people think, by the herd spirit, by the stereotype into which custom and prejudice try to fit us. We need quiet to keep in touch with ourselves, to recharge the soul that is uniquely ours. You need quiet to just be *you* rather than a straw man.

Many who are concerned about modern man view with alarm the collectivistic theories of society which contend that the greatest fulfillment is in submerging individuality in the mold of society. Such a way of life can create dark and twisting pressures on the unique minds of men, who need freedom to write their poems, build their bridges, compose their melodies, explore the land, the sea and the air. The discoveries that have lifted the human race have not come from planning commissions, committees, or conclaves. They have come from individuals who, in liberty and quietness, have drawn strength from their own selfhood. Forms of government that thwart such expression should be opposed.

But even under less extreme circumstances we face other, more immediate pressures, some more subtle than others, that impinge upon us all the time. Society is always squeezing us to live in a prescribed manner, to entertain like other

people, to vacation like everyone else—to look alike, to keep
up appearances comparable to our neighbors'.

Though some of these pressures prod us with demonic
subtlety, I was confronted with a none too subtle type a short
time ago when I was interested in buying an automobile.
After learning a bit about the price of new cars, I ruminated
silently that it would be fitting and proper to find a car of
1940 vintage that had been treated kindly by someone and
which could be obtained at a most moderate price before it
was put out to the junkyard pasture.

In the course of my shopping I came across an acquaintance who introduced me to a whole new vocabulary—that of
the used-car dealer. For your edification, he informed me
that a "pig" was a car that wasn't popular. It didn't sell
promptly. No one liked it. A "tomato" was one that had a
questionable background. You couldn't tell what might happen with it. The transmission could fall out or a wheel might
come off. But a "cream puff" was a satisfactory late-model
car.

Bearing the proper nomenclature in mind, I said firmly,
"Well, I've come to look, then, at your cheapest, nice, clean
'pigs.' "

My friend looked at me incredulously and said with great
earnestness, "Ditzen, you can't look at any 'pig.' You should
buy a new car."

I shook my head in definite negation, "That's out."

In confidential tones he pressed on. "Why, you're a pro-
fessional man, a member of dignified calling. You can't run
around in a 'pig.' After all, you wouldn't think of wearing a
dirty shirt. People judge you by the car you drive. You
couldn't go back to your community and let those nice people there see you driving on the street in a 'pig.' They'd be
ashamed of you. The very least you can do is to buy a 'cream
puff.' "

I confess that the wisdom and hard-to-come-by common

sense, gained in quiet, succumbed to the stereotype argument he presented. I fell into the trap of pride and rationalization that says, "You don't want to be out of step, or appear too different, or embarrass your children, etc., etc." And so I ended up driving away, not in the "best," but in a "fairly good" used "cream puff."

How real can be such pressures that plague us!

I recount that ridiculous incident because I hope it points up that we ought to do a lot more intelligent smiling at the foolish hurdles we jump in order to protect our precious egos from being bruised by others. What precious time we waste that could be used in the silent strengthening of our distinct selfhood.

It is the seed of quiet, and its fruit, that helps to develop a strong personality that can stand up masterfully to all kinds of pressures. Some months ago I met a most appealing Negro woman, who is employed by our State Department and is doing a wonderful job for our government and people in Asia. Drawn by her self-possession and dignity, I was interested to learn her background. She told me she, an orphan, had been raised by a wise and kind grandmother in a tiny Kansas town. That grandmother had been denied a formal education, but she had practiced the secret of the ancient prophet Isaiah: "in quietness and confidence shall be your strength." She had an inner calm from which came expressions of wisdom that went deep and remained forever with the little granddaughter who shared her life and love.

One thing she told the child was this: "Never let any outside slight or hurt or handicap get inside and stay to hurt you." The second thing the older woman counseled was: "Be what you are best intended to be. Be it in your soul! Break the stereotypes of what others think our people are."

The little girl who heard those words is now a strong and gracious woman, speaking impeccable English. Her voice is well modulated. Her enunciation is clear. She is well groomed, intelligent, self-possessed. What made her that way were insights from that older woman, who had won her wisdom in quietude and then inspired a little girl to grow into the unique human being she has become.

The development of a masterful personality is lopsided unless there is both a developing of and then a holding back of the reservoirs of quiet. The complete outpouring of our physical, emotional, and psychic energy into any task or cause leaves us hollow. The "reserving" of ourselves is basic to victory in life.

The most masterful personalities I have known have, in one way or another, kept their own counsel or deliberately retained their inner quietude. How often Jesus was quiet. The thirty "silent years" as they are called, when He lived with His parents in the hillside village of Nazareth above the plain of Esdraelon, were given over to long periods of silent thinking, of a steady communing with His own nature. That discipline gave Him confidence and strength for the years of public ministry. Above all, it provided Him with serenity and the assurance that tumultuous external perplexities would not be met with more noisy conflict. The means to their resolution lay in the depth and strength of His inner quietude.

The adage, "Speech is silver but silence is golden," points to an important aspect of the masterful personality. Considering this important quality led Carlyle to express it thus: "Speech is of Time, Silence is of Eternity," and led him to muse further on the individuals who have really made contributions to their societies. They were not the ones who spent themselves wastefully on the noisy inanity of the world. They were noble citizens of "the great Empire of Silence." "A country that has none or few of these is in a bad way. Like a forest which had no roots; which had all turned into leaves and boughs;—which must soon wither and be no forest. Woe for us if we had nothing but what we can *show,* or speak."

The most important thing about you is not the seen part. Not the man in a business or profession. Not the woman as homemaker, mother, participant in community affairs. The important thing is your relationship to the Empire of Silence.

I recall a conference with an ambassador of our country to a troubled area of the world. Afterward a publisher of discrimination who had been present commented, "What struck me was his silence. That man has inner reserves. I felt that strength. He'll do all right in his tough spot."

The same holds true for you and me. To do all right in the exacting task of living we need to cultivate our own inner quiet. Out of this comes the person who will be a victor in life. We are not masters but slaves if we sell our birthright of individuality for the mess of pottage called conformity.

There are times when we need the light touch, the capacity to "laugh off" unnecessary obligations, which we take on to keep up appearances. And there is warm satisfaction in directing our personality toward the goal for which it is best suited. But always preserve an area of deep seriousness, where your uniqueness is protected, where it cannot be pressured, or you will be lost. Here will lie your convictions, your deepest thoughts, your assurance of yourself and what is worthwhile.

In 1876 Thomas Huxley made an address at the convocation of Johns Hopkins University. In his speech he said that he was unimpressed with America's size or material achievements. "You and your descendants," he said, "have to ascertain whether this great mass will hold together under the forms of a republic (when) . . . population thickens in your great cities . . . and communism and socialism will claim to be heard . . ." Over eighty years ago he showed amazing insight into the course of history. But a more significant observation was this: *"The one great condition of success, your sole safeguard, is the moral worth and intellectual clearness of the individual citizen."*

Who will deny it? How can there be a free nation, a republic of order, unless there are individuals with intellectual clarity and who have, deep within themselves, come to an understanding of what is morally right and wrong and worthwhile? Ask next, how there can be a citizenry who will live by moral insight? How can there be people who do not merely repeat sentimentally a pledge of allegiance to the flag with the words, "liberty and justice for all," but also will see that it must be applied in their own lives? How can there be individuals who will not be swayed by prejudice, by noise, by mob violence? How else than in the foundations laid by individuals who also build within the quietude of their own minds and souls?

The tensions and the injustices existing in some of the Southern sections of our country are not held within by state lines. They are not isolated by geography. This whole people is bound up with what happens in any part of the nation. Although the whole world may observe this internal tension, quiet is heaviest on our own conscience, as a treason against God who made us equal, a treason against the most sacred principles we have as a people: "liberty and justice *for all.*"

How do we keep on an even keel? How rectify wrongs that have been done and are still being done? I'm convinced it's not by continued strife, bitter argument, recriminations. Nor by more rebelliousness and violence. It must come about by the communication of a conviction that an individual knows to be true. It reaches out silently and touches the mind and soul of another. It is gripping beyond argument. It is a final pronouncement that says, "The words *liberty* and *justice* have been inwardly heard and I know them to be right and true." This kind of confidence, this kind of self-mastery—

which refuses to be diluted or overcome by the problems it faces, which patiently, persistently, courageously strives to make our land more Christian and more truly American—comes from people who feel deeply, first of all, within their own quietude.

Introspection requires caution and balance, or it can become a dangerous thing. It is the means to a goal, not an end in itself. Many a mental patient, suffering from an illness known as schizophrenia, has become ill because he has refused to, or is unable to, maintain his way on the hard path of reality. He has sought escape in another world where he is safe from life's burdens and cares and can, in imagination, be free of all responsibilities. How much more desirable this is than struggling with an environment where there is always one difficulty or another, where you may fall on your face and have little in the way of achievement or distinction!

The way of health is neither living only on the outside nor withdrawal into the self. There must be a balance of both. "There must be a going to life," as the prophet Isaiah would say, "but ah, my friend, don't forget the returning and the rest. There is your saving." You come into the quietude of yourself that you may go to life again with confidence and strength.

Let's say to ourselves that there is a need for each of us to make experiments to learn how best to develop the resources of our own solitude. It's only by doing this that we gain our soundest understanding about God. That deep knowing is beyond what the preacher can say to us from the pulpit, or the theologian can put in his volume, or godly people can convey to us as we walk with them through life. The unshakable assurance that there is a purpose at the heart of all creation comes not by argument or logic. It is heard in the sound of eternity echoing in our soul.

But there must be receptiveness inside in order to hear the truth. The deep, inner knowing that we were made for harmony and not discord, that we were made to achieve peace and good will in the world, comes the same way, not from listening to the cries of the exterior world, with its many loud words lacking in meaning and its agitated activity of little worth.

You ask: How does one come to an understanding of God? By reading His word? Yes. By communication with others? Yes. But most effectively by developing an inner peace. Confidence that we came out of the heart of the Creating Power, that we were put here to build a useful and significant life, and that our spirit will be claimed at the end by Him who made us, opens the door to the noblest generosity that you and I can achieve. We gain a perspective on life and action toward life. It enables us to look on the world without frustration or bitterness or aimlessness. We see it as a place where our lives contribute meaning to creation and we are proud and happy to be alive.

Emerson, in his essay, "Uses of Great Men," speaks of his admiration for men of strength and eloquence who stand on "legs of iron," superbly fulfilling their mission in life, whether it be with the sword or the staff. Then he goes on: "But I find him greater when he can abolish himself and all heroes (and offices), by letting in this element of reason, irrespective of persons, this . . . irresistible upward force, . . . so great that the potentate is nothing." Then follows this wonderful sentence: "Then he is a monarch who gives a constitution to his people; a pontiff who preaches the equality of souls and releases his servants from their barbarous homages; an emperor who can spare his empire."

That kind of heroic living, that real greatness of spirit, of which we are all capable, comes from the individual who has returned to the source whence he came. And the path is through communion with one's heart, one of the surest roads leading to knowledge of God.

With knowledge of God comes richest kind of independence and freedom. Rudyard Kipling gave, in 1923, the Rectorial Address at St. Andrews University, Scotland, under the title "Independence." In it, amid many incisive and positive observations he affirmed: "Let the council of thy own heart stand, for there is no man more faithful unto thee than it. For a man's mind is sometime wont to show him more than seven watchmen who sit above in a high tower."

By independence I do not mean freedom from restraints or responsibilities. More importantly, I mean a harmony of outward action with inner integrity, joined by a humble but firm belief in what is right. A man speaking and acting in accordance with his beliefs will feel no fear, no shame, no regret. The opinions and acts of others have their place—but they cannot buy off the independent man or tarnish what he has found in his own quietude.

If we will but listen, we will hear the counsel that gives us confidence and strength from our inward voices, which are only heard in quietness and tranquillity. Here is a door to the understanding of God, the way to generous and useful outgoingness, to independence of spirit. This indeed is an added step on the road to self-mastery.

III

THE PLACE
OF FAITH
IN SELF-MASTERY

According to your faith be it done unto you.

Matthew 9:29

To fight out a war, you must believe something and want something with all your might. So must you do to carry anything else to an end worth reaching. More than that, you must be willing to commit yourself to a course, perhaps a long and hard one, without being able to foresee exactly where you will come out.

O. W. Holmes, Jr.

Faith is not belief in spite of evidence, but life in scorn of consequence—a courageous thrust in the great purpose of all things and pressing forward to finish the work which is in sight, whatever the price may be.

Kirsopp Lake

Faith is the force of life.

Tolstoi

Systems exercise the mind; but faith enlightens and guides it.

Voltaire

I swear I will never henceforth have to do
with the faith that tells the best!
I will have to do only with that faith that
leaves the best untold.

Walt Whitman

IN THE COURSE of the years I have talked to a number of people who have said, "I don't have any faith," or "I've lost my faith."

It's important to understand what is meant by the word "faith." Based on Latin and Greek derivations, our modern English word "faith" means "trust" or "belief." It implies unshakable persuasion about a person or a matter. It is used to describe a confidence that is indestructable, an assurance that is fused into the very nature of a person's being, as carbon is merged with iron to produce steel. If we use that word with such meaning, then we will reply to the individual who says he has no faith, "It isn't so! You have to have some faith to go on existing."

A woman years ago told me that she could not believe in God. To her, Jesus was merely a Palestinian teacher with visions of grandeur, around whom legend had grown up. The Church meant only pious mumbo-jumbo and hypocrisy.

"How about people?"

"Faith in them? Heavens no! There's no capacity for goodness in man. What keeps any semblance of decency and order," she went on to say, "is prohibitive law, romantic sentimentality, and the pressure of mediocre mores."

Recalling that someone had mentioned to me that she was interested in health and diet, I moved to that area. She swooped upon the new topic like a trout rising to a hatch of flies in the pool. The virtues of yogurt and wheat germ were

41

praised with the same definiteness that religion and all its trappings had been damned. It was like a crescendo in a symphony as she affirmed, "But it's really blackstrap molasses that holds the secret."

In mock amazement I said, "You don't mean to say that you have *faith* in that horrible-looking stuff?"

"I certainly do."

There has to be faith in something or we wouldn't take the next step or draw the next breath. At the end of the blackest, most aimless trail of despair and bitterness, a man, just to go on existing, must believe that it's better to be alive than dead.

In Graham Greene's play, *The Potting Shed,* one of the characters was James Callifer, a man who couldn't find meaning in anything. He says, "A room without faith . . . [is] . . . like a marriage from which love has gone. All that's left are habits and pet names and sentimental objects picked up on beaches and in foreign towns that don't mean anything any more. And patience, patience everywhere like a fog." But there had to be some faith in Callifer's life—if nothing more than the flickering hope that somewhere, somehow, there was some meaning—or he wouldn't have gone on.

Our real faith is not necessarily that which we put into words. It may not be found in our verbal professions. But whatever it is, it's the basis by which we live, whether it be adding blackstrap molasses to our diet or turning back from some chasm of futility to a plateau of hope.

Some people live by a growing confidence that God *is* and that they are His children. Some are held by the belief that there is no mastery in life unless we uphold certain standards of virtue. At every level it is faith of one kind or another that comes first.

The person who says that he has lost his faith, I often find, hasn't faced the fact that a healthy faith is a vital, a changing thing. It ought to be a growing experience. Many a young person needs to lose the belief that life was made for his pleasure and learn by experience that his pleasure is only found in serving his fellow man.

There may be someone reading these lines who still has a childish idea of God, which was never enlarged by mature thinking, which lacks relatedness to life's experiences. Many such individuals discard something valuable which needs only to grow with them.

No, don't say you've lost your faith. You may have lost some concept, which, like the butterfly that breaks from its cocoon, you have now outgrown. Ask yourself: Was it an adequate faith? Was it one that you could live by all the time? Letting it slip away can be the impetus for establishing a wider, finer structure of faith than you ever had before.

Theodore Beza said centuries ago to the King of Navarre, "Sire, it belongs . . . to the Church of God, . . . to receive blows and give them, but it will please your Majesty to take notice that it is an anvil which has wore out many hammers." It's basic to have something like that to build the masterful life. Faith must be like an anvil that can take life's blows. If it can't stand up to fate's events and circumstances, it is not adequate. Each of us needs a faith stronger than the impact of all the hammers of time and tragedy. To acquire it, there are some aspects of faith we likely should slough off.

When we talk about faith, we're talking about an active force. Like any energy, it needs to be replenished. It must be guarded and converted into life, just as the waters of a dam must be watched and channeled before being converted into the electricity that will illumine a city. Where there is such a dynamic faith, man may mold life according to his will.

This truth is powerfully expressed in many incidents in the Bible. One story tells of two blind men who appealed to

Jesus, desiring to have their sight restored. As the Master passed by they cried out, "Have mercy on us."

You might expect Jesus to reply, "Of course, I know you want to see. I sympathize deeply with the affliction that is yours. Your darkness is mine. Out of the light that comes from the Creator you now will see. Behold, your sight is restored!" No, He didn't say that at all.

Observe carefully. Jesus did not answer a word. He did not stop, but continued on, followed by a few curious ones, plus the loyal disciples who went with Him. After some time they came to a village and sought refuge for the night in a friendly house. The blind men had continued to follow Him during the long hours, their plea for mercy unfulfilled. Surely the Master had been aware of them all the time; apparently they had to do more than just wish and petition for their vision. The blind men, too, entered the house, and there, in the quiet, Jesus turned to them and asked, "Believe ye that I am able to do this?"

Jesus was searching deep into the hearts of these men. It was the crucial test of faith.

The blind men respond, "Yea, Lord."

Then touched He their eyes, saying, *"According to your faith be it done unto you."*

This is a spiritual force beyond all measure. It says, "If you deeply believe, if you have faith, life will be bent that way before you. Have first a faith that God made you to master life, and you will master be!"

Just wanting something, just desiring and thinking about it, wistfully dreaming, hopefully pleading, isn't enough! *You must really believe it is possible to achieve it, and you must follow your faith to wherever it leads.*

What we are talking about here is not just "blind faith." It does not avoid recognition of facts and use of good sense. Rather, it is built upon them. As J. P. Jacks, a principal at one of Oxford's colleges, expressed it, "Faith is reason grown courageous."

Some years back I, with other students of Norman E. Richardson, a wonderfully stimulating teacher, was engaged in some research that resulted in a volume entitled *Toward a More Efficient Church*. The purpose of the book was to guide parishes in developing a well-rounded congregational life. In the course of our studies we investigated the most significant symbols used across the centuries to portray Christian values. We found the symbol most frequently used for faith was an anchor. And it is easy to understand why.

Faith is not a burst of light that illuminates for a moment and then leaves us in darkness again. It is not something that can be imposed on us from the outside by authority. It isn't necessarily what we verbally confess in creed.

Rather it's an anchor that drags deep in the ocean of longing, feeling, perceiving. We can't completely see the bottom, but we know it is there. Our limited vision cannot penetrate that depth, but this we know: In the dark unseen, that anchor finds a lodging place. And in that firm holding, our acts of faith are confirmed. The anchor is tied to the ship of our life. Its value is beyond any price, because when the storms blow, it steadies the ship, saves it from destruction. We have courage to believe that the anchor will hold and that we will ride out any hurricane.

This dynamic faith gives above all else, an unshakable confidence in God's Providence. He rules. Although man doesn't understand the storm and cannot see the reason for its damage, faith in God creates calm in the heart.

Yes, faith *is* reason grown courageous. It requires faith to courageously affirm that what appears to be only turmoil has some part, a significant part, in bringing things more aright than ever before. Faith says, "All things—not just the 'nice' things, not just 'some' things—work together for good to those that love God."

The struggle for that faith at times may cause mental anguish and heartbreak. Bitter tears may flow. But faith is the anchor that will preserve us and strengthen us to humbly say: "Not my will but thine be done."

Some of the most thoughtful scholars of this generation have contended, as did Leslie Paul a few years ago in his book, *The Annihilation of Man,* that the violence of our times reflects man's revolt against the emptiness of a life that has lost such an anchor of faith. Leslie Paul was thinking of the faith that has produced the great principles of Western civilization: justice, mercy, freedom. These, he saw, are being undermined. They are tottering, and in many places we have seen them already crumble and fall before onslaughts of cruelty and terror. There is an absence of what Plato called "intellectual principle."

Examine the history of our Western civilization and you will see that its moral structure is the result of a faith born of the Greek, Jewish, and Christian traditions. Built into its core was a powerful faith in God and a faith in man. That faith has been weakened. For many it has become a habitual rather than an intellectual principle that holds life anchored securely against storms.

It was so with Germany in 1930. That nation epitomized the finest Western civilization—educated, scientific, cultured —going through all the customary, accepted motions of Christian doctrine and practice. But it was superficial gloss, concealing the fact that the honest values and principles in individuals and in the culture as a whole had become eroded. Let us never forget what happened there. It could happen elsewhere: treachery supplanting justice; mercy completely strangled by cruelty; the warmth of freedom enslaved in cold shackles; truth thrown from its place of pre-eminence, and King Lies, put in its place.

To master the twisting, chaotic forces that can destroy our

civilization, there has to be faith in—not lip service to—freedom and justice and mercy, the conviction that those qualities sprang from the heart that brought forth this vast and mysterious creation.

Sir Richard Livingston, a few years back, observed that every civilization grows up around a core of beliefs and values. Observing that when that healthy nerve becomes deadened, the culture decays and then dies, he turned to our modern life and saw that that is happening to us in the twentieth century. We have become, he contends, "a civilization of means without ends; with an ample body, but with a meagre soul; with a rich inheritance, but without clear values or a ruling principle."

Well, a culture, a civilization is made up of people, of individuals. And individuals who work at rebuilding a healthy faith in themselves, not only have an anchor for their own life; they also bring health to their civilization. To grow, then, in a vigorous faith is to provide a tonic for our sick times.

Now let us move to the important question of how to achieve the vigorous faith that means personal and social health.

We cannot gain a faith without continuous intellectual seeking and growing. The great enemies of faith, on any level, are suspicion and skepticism. You can have confidence in an individual, but let a cloud of suspicion about that individual enter your awareness and your faith in that individual lessens, perhaps dies. But more than that happens. Doubt is an insidious poison, which, like an infection, enters the body at one point and soon permeates the whole system.

Something must be immediately done when that virus enters our consciousness. One individual I know, who has developed a positive and healthy faith toward God and man and life, has told me that on any level—whether it be suspicion or disbelief regarding an individual or an idea—she immediately backs off to seek the facts and weighs the evidence. But most of all she puts suspicion aside and tries to place emphasis on what is positive.

If it is an individual who causes her doubt, she centers her thought and concern on the good qualities of that person. The intensity of her original faith may have to be modified; but on the other hand, by not unreasonably condemning the person because of some flaw, she brings balance to bear on her judgment.

To develop this evaluation of situations takes time; it requires the constructive and positive effort of observation, of honest appraisal and synthesis. But out of it emerges a new foundation for faith. And it usually produces a stronger, maturer, sounder faith.

To the individuals who have said, "I've lost my faith," I have on occasion replied, "Well, what are you doing about it?" If the good bucket that has carried water from the well develops a leak and doesn't hold water any more, the only way I know to make the vessel useful again is to plug up the hole. If that isn't satisfactory, how about getting another bucket? How foolish we are when in self-pity and doubt we mourn, "I have lost something," but then make no effort to go back over the path we traveled to determine where it was lost.

Years ago, in postgraduate work, a fellow classmate engaged in an action that I thought was reprehensible. Whereas he had been high in my estimation, he was now no "lower than mud." But I was unhappy in my feeling toward him; I found the incident troubling me in sleep. It made for embarrassing and unpleasant moments in our contacts together. After some time I decided to speak to him openly and frankly about the incident. Doing so gave him an opportunity to tell his side of the story. It so happened that his side revealed that I had misjudged him. Circumstantial evidence had altogether misrepresented the real facts of the case. With my faith in him restored and modified, our friendship was reestablished.

George Santayana wrote in a letter to William Lyon Phelps, "Faith is an assurance inwardly prompted, springing from the irrepressible impulse to do, to fight, to triumph." Such an assurance that pays off in successful living has to receive constant attention and care.

One of our finest satisfactions in life comes from what we create or do ourselves. Some time ago I visited the farm of a friend. The property was purchased already furnished with interesting items. My friend and his family had spent great effort to improve the property and to add to the hospitable furnishings. As we wandered through the rooms I felt that the keenest satisfaction was shown when we were shown what had been done with their own hands:

"We painted this room."

"You see that table over there. Our son made that in his woodworking class."

"I wish you could have seen this room before we took out the wall that was there. The whole family, working together, refinished the floors. Then we papered the walls and painted the ceiling." What had been done with their own effort was what was most meaningful.

The faith that is most meaningful to us has come from our effort and fashioning. As we use our own minds, make observations, and then crystallize judgment, we build up an inward treasure that gives us deep satisfaction.

One of the most helpful things we can do is to stimulate each other to think about and explore this area of belief and value judgments.

When I am asked to perform the marriage of young people, I make occasion to speak to them of the importance of working cooperatively together in all phases of life. From years of counseling with people who have difficulties in their marriage, I tell them the most important area of all is faith. The togetherness that really supports us in life doesn't come as we stand looking at each other but rather as, together, we look outwardly, at the abiding principles and values, the eternal truths. In talking together, in sharing the results of thinking and reading with one's mate or with a close associate or friend, both the foundation and the towers of one's faith are made firmer.

Many an individual grows in faith through the experience of private as well as public worship. In the long and bitter struggles of Holland to achieve its independence, there was one particularly dark period when the little nation seemed to be almost overwhelmed. In the heat of the conflict one of the generals of William of Orange sent a missive inquiring if he had achieved an alliance with England or France. Such an alliance would have provided much needed aid in those desperate hours. The reply of William is recorded thus: "You ask me if I have made a treaty for aid with any great foreign power; and I answer, that before I undertook the cause of the oppressed Christians in these provinces, I made a close alliance with the King of Kings; and I doubt not that He will give us the victory." The faith of William of Orange, which gave power and confidence to his words and actions, and which had a large part in the eventual victory for the Netherlands, is faith that you and I can experience in worship.

We permit ourselves at times to lead such mundane and grubby lives, carrying commitments from which we cannot escape. But we bend so heavily under them that we see nothing else. We are in danger of losing the sense of wonder and of awe, qualities indispensable to a great faith and a life of breadth and openness.

Go to church. Not critically, not with the feeling that you are there as a spectator. Go as a participator. The clergyman will have his inadequacies, the choir may sing off key, you may see people there whose actions outside that building are far from worthy. But don't let these matters trouble you. You are in a sacred place, a place where men and women have come through the centuries to pray to God.

No matter how humble the sanctuary may be, say to yourself that the doors of this place open onto the vast mystery of the meaning of all things. You are there humbly and receptively, opening your heart to it all. Sing the great hymns. Pray the prayers from the treasury of spiritual experience. Let your wonderment at your origin and your destiny rise on wings of faith. Let the people, the physical place, fall away, and you will add another dimension to experience to give inner support and outward power.

The matter of prayer, both personal and corporate, is an avenue for us to explore and cultivate as a means to a growing faith. As you think of God as being the spirit of perfect love and truth, harmony and peace, the spirit of creative compassion that enfolds all mankind and all creation, a breadth and depth will come to your mind and your soul as you meditate on that divine power and seek to stand in its presence.

In *The Struggle Within* Olgivanna Lloyd Wright attests, "We can magnetize and strengthen our faith with prayer. Prayer is a powerful emanation." That's true. As we engage in regular prayer, we bring into our person a peace and calm that counteracts worry and frustration.

Many are able to enrich their faith by reading the Bible and by renewing contact with the beginnings of our re-

ligious heritage. When I speak of reading the Bible I do not
mean to begin at the first chapter of Genesis and read the
entire book straight through. There is unquestioned merit
in that. Several lifetimes could be spent in studying the Bible,
and the spiritual treasures it possesses in every book would
not be exhausted.

But to develop faith, I think it best to select "a Bible
within the Bible." Read the Psalms, some of the great biographies of the Old Testament; the messages of the Prophets,
alight with insights; and, of course, the crowning revelations
in the New Testament; all are rich sources to stimulate the
mind and nourish the soul. The life and teachings of Jesus,
together with the chaste literary beauty of the Bible, will
bring you quiet and calm as well as faith.

There comes to my mind, among the many stories from the
Bible, the unforgettable one about the father and his de-
mented son. All the love and the misery of the parent's
thwarted hopes are felt in his words to the Master: "If thou
canst do anything, have compassion on us and help us." Jesus
responds to his heartrending plea, "If thou canst believe, all
things are possible to him that believest." You see what happened. The father is not merely a spectator; he is brought
into the activity, he is a participator. Jesus tells him that his
own belief, his cry for belief to overcome his unbelief, will
open the way to the power that conquers. With the father's
intense longing fused to unswerving faith, the Master is able
to restore the boy.

If there is to be any healing, any miracle wrought, any
movement forward, it takes more than mere vocal sentiment
or surface desire to turn the tide. Jesus has shown you the
way: Believe with such absorbed intensity, such unwavering
persistence, that every cell of your body, every impulse of
your mind, is concentrated toward the end you desire. And
each time you read the Bible the truth will be underlined

that faith is not passive resistance nor quiet waiting. It is an active, powerful force within you.

Association and friendship with people of faith is another way to grow in faith ourselves. How frequently it has been said, and rightly, that faith can't be taught; it has to be caught. The true spirit of wholesome faith is communicated to others, who in turn pass it on to those who come in contact with them.

One of the best examples over the centuries has been friendship with Jesus of Nazareth, the radiant source of motivating a faith that this world can neither give nor take away.

Create friendship with men like Socrates, Gandhi, Albert Schweitzer through their writing; some of their persuasions will fire your own convictions. I do not speak of such men with any intent or desire to exclude those who are living by our side daily. There are individuals of noble character and great capacity around us. Make occasion to meet them, be with them. They have something to give to us.

One of the values of seeking association with individuals of faith is the perspective and assurance we gain from them. You remember the childish story of the little chicken who, pausing under an oak tree, was bumped on the head by a falling acorn. Fear-struck, the little chick cried that the sky was falling. Similarly, left to our own devices, we can easily be thrown off on a tangent by the intrusions and pains of the day. But association with individuals who have, by meditation and experience, developed a more stable faith can help us to build our own more soundly.

Faith is developed too by acting on the basis of the knowledge and faith we have. George Buttrick put it, "We must live 'as if'—this requirement is levied on every realm of life. The scientist must experiment 'as if.' Those two little words are the synonym of hypothesis, and science proceeds by hypotheses. The scientist does not know the inmost nature that his diagnosis is correct: the highway to knowledge is to act 'as if.' "

You have, let us say, a feeling that men are basically good. It is not a firmly set faith yet, but if you act as though it were true, you will find that the belief is settling down more and more into a solid foundation for some of your deepest convictions. You will find that men are good.

David Livingston said, speaking of faith, "It requires perpetual propaganda to attest its genuineness." That is the final point to remember. You do not grow in faith merely by discussing it abstractly, by playing with one possibility and then another. You grow into it by affirming it, by *living* it. Take a firm stand on a conviction and say, "I will look on life, and act in life, as though this were final truth." Doing that, you will find that it is so and your faith will be strengthened. Or you will find that it is not altogether so and you will need to stand more firmly until you have won.

As you work at it, yours will be the conviction that life can be molded after your faith. That is one of the most powerful thoughts and truths in all human experience, put with beautiful simplicity by Jesus: *"According to your faith, be it done unto you."*

IV

HANDLING

THE DIS-EASE OF

TENSION

For everything there is a season, and a time for every purpose under heaven.

Ecclesiastes 3:1

I have seen the travail which God hath given to the sons of men to be exercised therewith.

Ecclesiastes 3:10

Sufficient unto the day is the evil thereof.

Matthew 6:34

The superior man is always candid and at ease with himself or others; the inferior man is always worried about something.

Confucius

O God, in restless living
We lose our spirits' peace
Calm our unwise confusion,
But Thou our clamor cease.
Let anxious hearts grow quiet,
Like pools at evening still,
Till Thy reflected heavens
All our spirits fill.

Harry Emerson Fosdick

After all, after all we endured, who has grown wise?
We take our mortal momentary hour
With too much gesture, the derisive skies
Twinkle against our wrongs, our rights, our power,
Look up the night, starlight's a steadying draught
For nerves at angry tension.

Robinson Jeffers

The truly wise man must be as intelligent and expert in the use of natural pleasures as in all the other functions of life. . . . Relaxation and versatility, it seems to me, go best with a strong and noble mind, and do it singular honor. There is nothing more notable in Socrates than that he found time, when he was an old man, to learn music and dancing, and thought it time well spent.

Montaigne

Every adult who reads these lines knows that one of the portentous problems for modern man in the Western world is to master the tensions that destroy efficiency, that cause dis-ease and death.

Says John A. Schindler, M.D., "A big textbook of medicine, such as medical students use, contains the account of roughly 1,000 different diseases. Emotionally induced illness is as common as all the other 999 put together.

"In 1951 a paper from the Yale University Out-Patient Medical Department indicated that 76% of patients coming to that clinic were suffering from (what the medical profession calls) emotionally induced illness." And in the southern part of our country, New Orleans' Ochsner Clinic reported that of 500 consecutive patients who were admitted to the department that handles gastrointestinal disease, 74% were suffering from emotionally induced illness.

And the cause? The medical profession, using laymen's language, says that it results, with scattered exceptions, from some form of needless tension.

It is not the natural tautness of the animal alert and aquiver in the presence of danger. Neither is it the concentration of the animal as it stalks its prey until the need of hunger is filled. Rather, it's a destructive tension that is continuous, that pounds the victim after the factory whistle blows, after the appointed hours for work are ended.

A friend who has been helpful in the ever-so-slight steps I

57

have made in the art of living, calls this "spinning the wheels." It's like the automobile on an incline, when the street is hard packed with wet snow. The motor races and roars. The rear wheels spin. But all that comes from it is terrific strain on the engine and burning of the tires. The vehicle doesn't get anywhere.

"I have seen," says the Old Testament Book of Ecclesiastes, "the travail which God hath given the sons of men to be exercised therewith."

In our generation it is tension that puts the travail upon us. Many of us are too often like the fighter who is punch-drunk. An injury has deadened his sense of when to stop. The bell rings to end the round, but he still goes on flailing the air, pouring out his energy, swinging and punching—all to no avail.

Of course, there's another side to this matter of tension. Ask yourself if you ever saw a tense turnip. To my knowledge a dandelion never had a nervous breakdown or the equivalent in the vegetable kingdom of that all too familiar ailment of genus Homo sapiens, stomach ulcers.

Jesus gave us a lovely illustration: the lilies of the field which "sow not, neither do they spin. Yet Solomon in all his glory was not arrayed like one of these." That picture is good for us to keep in mind. Perhaps there are times when it could help us ease unnecessary strains we put on ourselves. But those gracious lilies do not have to face what man does—a world where there are choices and decisions, where there are responsibilities and moral consequences, where there is opportunity as well as a need for spiritual questing and intellectual growth.

God created the lilies of the field. But the Bible also tells us that when man was made, God breathed into him His own breath, His own spirit. So a consciousness different from a possible consciousness of the lily was instilled in him. It was an awareness of a world in which there is value, one in which some things are more significant or important than others. A world in which man could drift aimlessly, but where also he could gird himself to struggle against the tide. God gave His crowning creation an awareness of the heights of good but also the depths of evil.

As that spirit was breathed into man there was created too a capacity to respond or not respond. Then, as surely as night follows day, tension was bound to exist too.

It became necessary at times to be taut, to stand tense and inflexible. In the southern part of France, where the Protestant Huguenots were imprisoned during the long black night of religious persecutions, there is, I'm told, a single word scratched in the stone floor of a prison cell. It was the work of many years, done with the fingernails of a prisoner. Through long months the soft nail scratched at the unyielding stone this one terrible, inspiring, awesome word, for all to see: RÉSISTE. There is great loss if man neglects his powerful capacity to resist injustice or mediocrity. He loses, and so does the world, if he cannot marshal his inner resources and become tense in a struggle for something better. And how important it is to use this power well, to keep it in its place.

The market is glutted with all kinds of advice telling us how to achieve this worthy end. Bookstores and newsstands, with their many books, papers, and periodicals devoted to the problem, give proof of a real need. Much of the advice I've read is good, but some of it seems pathetically shallow. Many times we're told that if we can just keep a pleasant frame of mind, make a game of living, turn our work into play, be at ease, take things a little more "in stride," stop striving too hard, get away from the sharp competitive struggle that tears us apart, all will be well. God knows we could apply much of this with profit.

In the fifteenth century Erasmus was giving to the people

of his time a similar kind of advice as he wrote, "After you have din'd, either divert yourself at some Exercise, or take a Walk, and discourse merrily, and Study between whiles . . . A little before you go to sleep read something that is exquisite, and worth remembering; and contemplate upon it till you fall asleep . . ."

But such advice wears pretty thin after trying it out for a while. Certainly Erasmus' counsel will seem archaic for many, as its modern form will seem watered down. It's all right to say, "I'm going to whistle a tune and take my job with a song and dance." But there are times when whistling and dancing are out of place and inadequate to the situation that has to be met. It's all well and good to preach to ourselves about keeping the light touch. Smile to yourself as you say, "I may end up in the poorhouse but I'm going to have a good time getting there and I'll live to sing at the funerals of the poor devils who beat me up the ladder." But when the going gets really tough and the demands heavy, this turns out to be an inadequate solution. The hunter, in tiger country, should have more than a peashooter.

One needs a heavy weapon to bring down big game. The complexities and pressures of modern life make formidable beasts. The counsel that says, "Keep the light touch" is firing with that peashooter when a monster is charging.

That is why the Bible is more helpful than many of our modern prescriptions and panaceas. It's realistic. It's balanced. Always positive and constructive, it yet knows the negative and destructive forces man must face.

Nowhere does the sacred record tell us we can walk along a perpetual path of sunshine, where inner lightheartedness can compliment the perennial flowers along the way. "There is a time for every purpose under the sun . . . . there is a time for war." There is a time for tension, for mobilizing our vital energies for the task. But the Bible goes on to affirm that there is another side too. "There is a time for peace." There is a time when the conflict is over, when the demands ought to be light, when the call for sacrifice and effort is negligible.

There will always be issues that have to be decided, momentous challenges flung at us, wrongs around us that need to be righted. What will we do in the face of them? Will we just view life pleasantly? Will we be passive? Neutral? No, there is a time for peace and its pleasantness, and we will rest and gain strength back while "God's in His heaven, All's right with the world." But when called, we will not fail in our obligation to face issues, accept challenges, right wrongs.

Something of that balance is expressed in the amusing anecdote about a man who had a long and rugged period of highly pressured work. Finally the time came for him to leave for his vacation.

"What are you going to do?" an acquaintance asked.

"I'm going to find a little cabin on a lake," was the response. "I'm going to put a rocking chair on the front porch. Then I'm going to sit and for a week do nothing."

"That's interesting," was the response. "After the week is up what then?"

"Well," was the reply, "I might start—just a little bit, mind you—but I might start *rocking*."

Perhaps you are thinking, "This discussion doesn't help me. I have such terrific responsibilities, and there's nothing I can do about it. The organization with which I am associated is so complex. We're going through continual changes and I just can't get away from it. I'm an engineer, or I'm a wife and mother, trying to run the seven-ring circus called the modern home, or I'm in sales and I have to keep the pressure on every minute."

The tensions borne by women are as acute as those of men. Managing a household, being cook and chauffeur and dishwasher and glamour girl, participating in the church fair, the P.T.A., and collecting for the Red Cross, put on pressures that are very real. Such an individual could possibly be saying, "I have so much to do. I certainly know about the necessary warring to get accomplished all that needs doing. But I can't, as much as I'd like to, get into my life the other side of the picture, the time for peace. I can't read poetry or raise roses or what-have-you."

If that thought is somewhere in the back of your mind, tell yourself right now that such a thought is a sin against the intelligence God gave you. It's sin against your body that was made to house your mind and spirit. You *can* make headway, and you must, in balancing the scales!

We may get to the top of some mythical ladder of achievement. But in our deepest selves we know that the crowning achievement won't be ours if, somewhere along the way, we haven't first mastered the pounding of the tensions that send us to doctors with all kinds of complaints and ailments. Those men so often understand the real cause of our pain, our ache, or our "dragginess." They don't have the time to counsel us to the point where they can lay bare the cause of the dis-ease for us. If they could, we would see tension which we had not mastered.

But we ourselves can do something about it. When we start packing the brief case to take home at night or for the week end, we can pack it full, put it at the side of the desk, then go to the door, open it, lock it, and walk away empty-handed.

Some evening, as you ride home on the train, rather than reading of juvenile delinquency in the late evening edition, just don't buy a paper at all. Don't talk to anyone about the drop in the stock market. Don't permit your spirits to get lower and your blood pressure higher.

Begin that book on how to tie flies. Remember you promised yourself last summer that you would. Check out of the luncheon that is a committee meeting. When you leave the office, avoid the trap of "shooting the breeze about what has to be done tomorrow" over what a cartoonist called the "triple-cocktailed nirvana." Rather, be a *character!* (That phrase, "be a character," is a significant one.) Be an individual. Go to a park bench or the library or a museum.

Use a little time, as you go to work in the morning, to think of the many and varied people who make your city. Ask how much you know about your town other than the sidewalk you pound from the station to your place of employment. And to get a change of pace, how about finding some answers to the questions that occur to you? It probably will turn out to be fun and full of surprises.

If we take on more than we should, we are like the little boy at the picnic who lustily gobbled six hot dogs. He may try to forget them as he runs on the beach. But his digestive system, working overtime, won't let him forget them. "Two hot dogs, eaten slowly, would have been better, Johnny," we, in great wisdom, inform the boy. We should remember such horse-sense counsel at 3:00 A.M. while we're still churning over yesterday's two committee meetings, and the special conference with the boss, the dinner date, telephone calls, and dictation that we face tomorrow.

We begin to fashion the shaft of balanced self-mastery as we realistically, honestly, and in terms of our own individuality say, "With God's help and my own intelligence, there is going to be peace as well as war. There has to be both in my life. I may not be able to escape the former, but I will not let the latter escape me."

Then that shaft of realism must be joined to the hub. There's no ultimate conquering of our tension, no balance of abiding peace, if we don't maintain contact with God.

If there is an infection in our bodies, the forces of healing automatically marshal themselves to combat it. We have also been given a mind and a moral sense to combat the dis-ease of tension, which is just as insidious as any virus that can get into our bodies. We possess resources, mentally and spiritually, that will control the dangers of tension, just as we have white corpuscles that fight germs. The difference is that the process is not wholly automatic, as it is with our physiological make-up. The mind and the soul need some source of power that will release our resources. The power that does it is the awareness and presence of God within you. This creative and creating power moves through all things and seeks to move through your life to give it order and power and balance and peace.

Rheinhold Niebuhr, one of the significant theologians of our day, has made the point several times that there is an "inevitability of tension." Caught in the web of original sin, we yet long for a better world and better life, which is denied us by the existence of personal and social sin. So we are inevitably strained and pulled by our own imperfect nature, a moral world, and aspirations that cannot be fulfilled. Niebuhr, with the profoundest philosophers and theologians of the ages, affirms that the only answer that can be helpful is the grace of God. God's forgiveness, His love, coming into our souls, will, as nothing else can, break the shackles of tension and bring restorative peace.

You may read that statement and say, "It's interesting. I've heard it since childhood. It's a difficult concept to grasp. Maybe it's helpful to someone else, but it hasn't done a thing for me." Its meaning will remain obscure if you think and talk that way. But if you consider it carefully, experiment with it often, one day you will come to know its cleansing, redemptive power and its true meaning.

There may be someone you don't know who loves, admires, respects you very much. But it will do you little good until you know about it, until you seek it out, until you believe it, until you can reciprocate with affection and regard and respect. So it is here. The healing from the most profound power in all existence, which can bring us into balance, will come only as we seek it, grow in believing it, accept the love and respect and give our devotion in return.

I can almost hear someone saying, "This matter of tension has been rehashed so often, in so many ways, and I still don't have anything that I can really lay my hands on that will help me. The concept of God is as vague as ever. Can't you be more specific?"

I think I can. Here is a simple suggestion, which has been helpful to me and others have told me has helped them reach a measure of peace when they were all twisted up with tension. One of the best-loved hymns of the church, "Dear Lord and Father of Mankind," by John Greenleaf Whittier, contains two stanzas that I suggest you commit to memory or write out on a card to carry daily in your wallet or purse. At least once in the day (always try to begin in the morning before the load of work is on your shoulders) read or repeat the lines. Do it slowly, savoring the thought, the beauty of language. Let the ideas sink deep into your consciousness to help you on the road to self-mastery:

> Dear Lord and Father of mankind
> Forgive [my] foolish ways
> Reclothe [me] in [my] rightful mind
> In purer lives thy service find,
> In deeper reverence praise.

> Drop thy still dews of quietness
> Till all [my] strivings [all the tensions] cease;
> Take from [my] soul the strain and stress,
> And let [my] ordered life confess
> The beauty of Thy peace.

V

MASTERY
THROUGH OUR
IDEAL SELF

And Jesus entered and passed through Jericho. And, behold, there was a man named Zaccheus, which was the chief among the publicans, and he was rich . . . And he ran before, and climbed up into a sycamore tree to see him . . . And when Jesus came to the place, he looked up, and saw him, and said unto him, Zaccheus, make haste and come down; for today I must abide at thy house.

Luke 19:1-5

Our ideals are our better selves.

A. Bronson Alcott

The situation that has not its duty, its ideal, was never yet occupied by man. Yes, here, in this poor miserable, hampered, despicable actual, wherein thou even now standest, here or nowhere is thy ideal; work it out therefrom, and, working, believe, live, be free. Fool! the ideal is in thyself.

Carlyle

At some time in our life we feel a trembling, fearful longing to do some good thing. Life finds its noblest spring of excellence in this hidden impulse to do our best.

Robert Collyer

Great people and champions are special gifts of God, whom He gives and preserves; they do their work, and achieve great actions, not with vain imaginations, or cold and sleepy cogitations, but by motion of God.

Martin Luther

The difference between one man and another is by no means so great as the superstitious crowd suppose.

Macaulay

Ah—the thrill of wrestling with dreams forever beyond us.

Anzia Yezierska

O<small>NE OF THE REASONS</small> some of us don't become masters of our lives is that we let the best, the ideal self that we were intended to be, become thwarted for any one of a hundred and more reasons. It may be held down or held back by circumstances, suffocated by events, put off the track by the expectation of others, but no matter what the cause, we suffer from inner dissatisfaction and frustration.

Some light is shed on this situation from an incident described in the Book of Luke. The place was Jericho. What does that name mean to you? The geographer and geologist might be interested in the fact that Jericho, near the Dead Sea, is 825 feet below sea level. It is interesting to the archeologist as the site of civilizations that go back to six thousand years before Christ, and earlier. To the sociologist, humanitarian, and political strategist, its large modern population of displaced Arabs from Israel is a matter of concern. The historian of the Roman Empire cannot avoid the name Jericho, because it is associated with the names of Roman conquerors and emperors: Bacchides, Aristobulus, Pompey, Vespasian, among others. Herod the Great built a winter palace at Jericho and seemed to hope it would become a famed winter resort, a fame that has not been realized.

And, of course, the biblical historian is interested in the place. He will tell you, from his knowledge of biblical references, that there are associations in Jericho with Joshua, the strong military leader of the wandering Israelites, and also

69

with the prophet Elisha. It was at Jericho that King Zedekiah was defeated by the Babylonian army, at which time the kingdom of Judah came to a bloody and tragic end.

I've seen Jericho in recent years. In memory three things stand out. One, the Arab women with their lovely flowing robes, carrying water pots on their heads with stately grace. Two, the fascinating excavations at Jericho, revealing layer after layer of fragments from civilizations that are no more, as the archeologist dug deeper and deeper. And three, a sycamore tree which was pointed out as the one where Zaccheus climbed to look down on the Master when He came to that town.

It behooves the modern traveler to examine some of the landmarks. I wondered, as I looked at that tree, if it could have been alive for two thousand years. Was it truly the tree into which Zaccheus climbed and whose branches shaded for a moment the most compelling spirit of history as He paused beneath it?

I confess to a rather suspicious reaction to specific sites, such as that one, particularly after being told of an incident in Egypt. Travelers near the pyramids of Giza, seeing the Nile some distance away, asked if Moses was taken out of the bulrushes in that area. Their guide responded, "Well, it used to be farther up the Nile. But we've moved it nearer for the convenience of the tourists." How could one be sure that this really was the tree Zaccheus climbed? But any doubt on that score could not suppress the thoughts that came to mind, just being there.

But Jericho's widest fascination is due to the fact that Jesus *was* there and that He centered His attention on one man, Zaccheus. The aura of eternity about Jericho comes from the fact that that man, caught by the attention of Jesus, found the sense of his best self and he began living again by that.

Sometimes it surprises me to realize that for eight years I have been minister to a wonderful congregation in Bronxville, New York. In listening to many a sermon, they have heard me at times repeat myself. It's bound to be that way, because there are certain sources that each of us go back to time and time again. When "the square pegs won't seem to go in any of the right holes," as someone put it, when the mind needs refreshment or stimulation, I go first to the Bible and then to one of a group of great spirits—Emerson, Thoreau, Shakespeare, Carlyle, William James. In preaching, as in writing this volume, I rely heavily on them and either consciously cite them or unconsciously express their thoughts. On the basis of what I find meaningful, I'm impelled to share it with others, in the hope that it may be helpful in some measure.

William James once said that he had many possible selves, many different identities, he would like to fulfill. That is probably the case with all of us. He wrote that he'd like to be "both handsome and fat and well-dressed, and a great athlete, and make a million a year, be a wit, a bon-vivant, a lady-killer, as well as a philosopher; a philanthropist, statesman, warrior, an African explorer, as well as a 'tone-poet' and saint. But," he added, "the thing is simply impossible."

Then he went on to speak of the fact that every man and woman, among the several selves that he or she might be, at some point has to decide which self will be the deepest, the truest one. For example, in the minister there may be still the latent Arctic explorer. In order to keep the one from causing frustration and unhappiness because it cannot be realized, and to keep the primary one faithful to its duty and commitments, there has to be some final decision. We must "pick out the one," says James, "on which to stake [our] salvation." When we do that, from that time on, the fortunes of this self, whatever it is, are very real. The defeats will be very real, bringing deep distress or shame, but the victories will bring the richest happiness and fulfillment to offset the defeats.

What happens to some of us is that our realest self, potentially, gets lost or is forced into a mold of somebody else's choice. Regardless of the causes or the blame, this self, facing difficulties at every turn, is held back and repressed.

I think it was that way with Zaccheus. He was a business man—a successful one. He bore the title, "Chief among the publicans," which suggests that he probably had immediate communication with the bureau of collections at Rome. Jericho was the center of a profitable balsam trade at this period of history. Quite likely, Zaccheus was the first tax officer, with a number of collectors under him, responsible for paying to Rome the required sum levied on the district of Jericho. Such a job was not one calculated to win friends. The chief collector had to be tough. If he was honorable, as I believe Zaccheus sincerely intended to be, he had to guard against bribery and overcharging and extortion among his subordinates. On the other hand, he had to be strict in collecting the payments, which many people found difficult to meet. The position was one that made it possible for a man to become wealthy, and Zaccheus took advantage of the opportunity.

But that wasn't the most significant thing about him. Zaccheus was basically and potentially what everyone wants to be: a sensitive human being, desiring to be helpful and a man of good will toward his fellow men. He wanted both to give and to receive respect and affection. He had within himself an ideal self that he longed to be, outgoing and selfless and generous.

But the tax-collecting business seemed to force him more and more into another, unpleasant kind of self, where he was forced to be close-mouthed, hard-handed, thinking of himself first and last. It was that man who climbed the sycamore tree to see Jesus.

Jesus came. I think the decisive thing that happened to Zaccheus was that he saw again the image of his best self. When Jesus showed him confidence and love, Zaccheus suddenly found the fortitude and courage to say, "This is the me that I want to be," and to do something about it. He vowed, "I'm going to give half my goods to the poor and if I've wronged anyone, I will pay him back fourfold."

That ancient but ever-new Bible story emphasizes that there cannot be deep contentment and full mastery until we act in accord with our best selves. In Mika Waltari's book, *The Egyptian,* the physician Sinuhe, a follower of the religion of Aton, returned, after a long absence, to his native soil and sought out an acquaintance by the name of Kaptah. This friend, a man who has adjusted completely to the world, said to the physician, "Nothing in the world is perfect. The crust of every loaf is burned, every fruit has its worm . . . For this reason there is no perfect justice; even good deeds have evil consequences, and the best motives may lead to death and defeat . . ."

Then he added, "Look at me, my lord Sinuhe! I am content with my mean lot and grow fat in harmony with gods and men . . . Take life quietly; it is not your fault that the world is as it is . . . that has ever been so and ever will!"

His friend Sinuhe reluctantly, sadly agreed. "Be it as you say," he replied. "I will ply my trade, and as a recreation I will also start some collection as you have counseled me."

The next day he received many lavish gifts from Kaptah. But Sinuhe mused at their reception and at a hunger they did not fill: "He sent me munificent presents, which secured for me such comfort and plenty that *nothing would have been wanting to my happiness, if I could have been happy."*

For that man, as for many, there can be no happiness, no inner glow that comes with the sense of knowing what is

right, what is best for him, when he was overwhelmed by an
alien society! To take Kaptah's advice was to compromise, to
adjust and forget his religion, to take things as they were—
this but created shame and hurt.

The longer I live, the surer I am that man is inwardly
stamped with an image of the ideal of what he ought to be
and is capable of becoming. Outward events and appearances
and actions do not necessarily destroy that ideal self. To deny
it, ignore it, try to forget it, to act in opposition to its claims,
is to have no anchor, no roots, to bobble and be without
purpose, losing the chance to master life fully.

There is a beautiful conversation from the *Dialogues of
Mortality,* which reads as follows:

> "The sheening of that strange bright city on the hill, barred
> by its high gates . . ."
>
> "Barred from all, Phrastes?"
>
> "From all, Eroton, who do not desire to enter it more
> strongly than they desire all other cities."
>
> "Then it is barred indeed, and most men must let it go."
>
> "Those who have once desired it cannot let it go, for its light
> flickers always on the roads they tread, to plague them like
> marsh fires. Even though they flee from it it may drag them
> towards it as a magnet drags steel, and though they may never
> enter its gates, its light will burn them with fire, for that is its
> nature."
>
> "Who then were the builders of this dangerous city?"
>
> "Gods and men, Eroton; men seeking after gods, and gods
> who seek after men. Does it not appear to you that such a
> fabric, part artifact and part deifact, reared out of divine inti-
> mations and demands, and out of the mortal longings and
> imaginings that climb to meet these, must perpetually haunt
> the minds of men, wielding over them a strange, wild power,
> intermittent indeed, but without end? So, anyhow, it has al-
> ways proved."

Yes, there is a strange and perpetual haunting of the person each of us was meant to be, at our best. And there's no

joy or peace until our daily acts are aligned harmoniously with it.

To do this, choices must continually be made. David Seabury in his book, *The Art of Selfishness,* pointed out that there is a good selfishness and there is an evil selfishness. There are compelling forces that can make for evil selfishness and those that can make for good selfishness. It's up to us to evaluate and then decide between them. For instance, there is the compelling force to withdraw. This, Dr. Seabury says, can be an evil side of selfishness. But its opposite is good: out-goingness. Intolerance is evil, tolerance and understanding good. You have the choice to make with every human being —whether it be the milkman or your mate, the janitor or your boss.

To achieve mastery in life, we must start, hour by hour, day by day, to evaluate on one side of the ledger or the other our actions in life's situations. Each time we are able to place our thoughts and behavior on the credit side, we bring more fully into existence the person who is our ideal within.

Occasionally I have time only for a hurried sandwich at a local drug store. One of the clerks is especially courteous, cheerful, and kind; his warm hello and pleasant chitchat are as nourishing to the spirit as the food is to the body. When I ask for extra mayonnaise or another glass of water, there's always prompt service, a smile, and "It's a pleasure to serve you."

Once I said to him, "I don't come in here often, but when-ever I do I'm always impressed with your pleasant attitude and thoughtful service. I'm grateful for it. I want you to know it's been helpful to me, as I'm sure it is to many others. I'd like to ask, if you wouldn't mind, two questions. First, are you this way day in and day out?"

He smiled as he kept an eye on possible needs of other lunchers to the right and left. "Not always. But I keep trying.

I figure most everybody is nice. The only way to act is so they'll feel you really believe that. Now and again a customer is disappointing. But I say to myself: 'Most aren't like that.' And it's true, they aren't."

"Well, from what I've seen, you have a good batting average. The other question is this, what helps you most to keep up your good spirits?"

"Don't know, other than the thought that life's too short to mess it up with meanness and irritation. I try to remember what my dad told me: 'Son, you can be a stinker, or you can be something better.' Guess that's pretty much it: I try to be better."

If we give in to the lesser, meaner self, we not only add to the negative side of life for others. We deny ourselves a precious ingredient to good living: a feeling of self-esteem. We may not be able to control the weather or setbacks and troubles that occur in the course of a day. But we can do something about controlling ourselves. If nothing more, we will have at any day's end the second essential ingredient: self-respect.

We must admit the fact that our best intentions don't always succeed. You and I can try, we can create the framework and be willing to strive—but still we falter, we fail, we sin. Louis Mumford defined sin as a defiance of what a man knows to be best. Sin isn't merely breaking rules that are established by the community, nor is it only deviation from the code of mores of a group. It is defying, not living by, what we inwardly know to be best. The discouraging but stubborn fact is that, in spite of our highest intentions, we do just that.

We all find that in trying to develop our best self, the lesser selves get in the way. I recall the incident told about Toscanini, who was unable to get the proper tone he wanted from one of the men in the orchestra. He raged bitterly at the man until his anger was spent. Later, other musicians told Toscanini that he was unduly severe with the man, who was a good musician and a man of integrity and character. At the next rehearsal, so the story goes, Toscanini apologized, saying he was sorry for losing his temper. But, as he talked, the memory of the incident rose again in his mind and he grew irritated. Remembering how he had struggled to bring to life that musical ideal, he shouted, "The trouble is God tells me how, but you, you, get in His way."

We often feel the urge to try our wings, but laziness or little setbacks stymie us. We give up, settle down comfortably again. At such times we know what's right, we know what our best self ought to be and could be—God tells us—but our lesser selves bog us down.

I have spoken little about the large goals, which involve the well-being of mankind. But I suggest now that identifying with some greater cause is an effective method to counteract laziness, or selfishness, or lack of purpose in life.

You are in business. Why? For what purpose? You are a homemaker or a grandmother. Again, what is your broader purpose, the goal for which you are working?

If your answers are merely "To make a living, to achieve success, to run an ordered home, to raise my children," you are missing out on some of the greatest satisfactions and achievements that man can know.

There is a definite and ever-present need to be aligned with purposes above and beyond ourselves. Be a businessman to increase the prosperity of mankind, or a mother who through her life and life of her children will make this a more peaceful world tomorrow than it is today, and you will be rising above the everyday, humdrum activities that never enrich man's spirit. Awareness of horizons far beyond us, toward which we are moving, will free us of the demons that shrivel our soul—envy, vanity, self-pride, the thirst for recognition and fame. Once rid of their drains and demands, we enter the ranks of those who are one with all mankind.

Such a man is a friend of mine. He is married, father of three children; an insurance salesman. He and his family live in a moderate-sized community typical of a thousand scattered across the country. His house is modest and no more conspicuous than that of his neighbors'. To all outward appearance it blends, as does his life, into the quiet and restricted environment. Yet you cannot be with him five minutes without feeling a sense of expansiveness. There is a breadth to his thinking and living. International law and order have claimed his interest increasingly since college days. He is an alert student of educational trends and participates in wider movements to improve education in America. His work is not just a business or a means of livelihood; it is a channel for offering practical help and genuine service to others. Because of his wider concerns he has facets of mastery that endow his life and affect all who know him.

Jesus offered Zaccheus forgiveness, love, that day as he passed through Jericho. That isn't an isolated experience that took place nineteen centuries ago in some little town near the Dead Sea. It's one that we can have today. Jesus passes through our lives, and His love, His compassion, and His trust reach out to enfold and lift us.

Above all else, there is hope and encouragement as we travel the road to self-mastery, because He gives us, or returns to us, the picture of our best selves and the assurance and strength to seek it.

VI

MASTERING
THE HOBGOBLIN
OF FEAR

I will fear no evil, for thou art with me.

Psalms 23:4

Our fears do make us traitors.

Shakespeare

Fear is a kind of bell, or gong, which rings the mind into quick life and avoidance upon the approach of danger. It is the soul's signal for rallying.

Henry Ward Beecher

I call that mind free which, through confidence in God and in the power of virtue, has cast off all fear but that of wrong doing, which no menace or peril can enthrall, which is calm in the midst of tumults, and possesses itself though all else be lost.

William Ellery Channing

We must be afraid of neither poverty nor exile nor imprisonment; of fear itself only should we be afraid.

Epictetus

The dove, O hawk, that has once been wounded by the talons, is frightened by the least movement of a wing.

Ovid

Unless you put a stop to your insatiate desires and quit yourself of fears and anxieties, you are but decanting wine for a man in a fever.

Plutarch

It is only the fear of God that can deliver us from the fear of man.

John Witherspoon

ON JANUARY 18, 1912, Captain Robert Falcon Scott and four companions reached the South Pole, only to learn to their dismay that they had been beaten in that world-shaking discovery by another explorer named Amundsen. Already the five had faced devastating hardship. They turned back. But severe weather conditions, sickness, and insufficient food made their travel extremely slow, bringing their bitter journey to a halt. Ten months later a search party found Scott's little tent, housing his body and those of his companions.

In that tiny speck of tent on that harsh and barren land the rescuers gathered together notes, letters, diaries that Scott had written. Among the last things Scott recorded, with hands so cold that he could barely hold a writing instrument, were these: "I do not regret this journey. We took risks; we knew we took them. Therefore we have no cause for complaint.

"Had we lived, I should have had a tale to tell of the hardihood, endurance, and courage of my companions which would have stirred the heart of every Englishman."

He left a letter, among others, to an old friend, Sir James M. Barrie, in which were these words: "Good-bye. I am not at all afraid of the end . . . We are in a desperate state, feet frozen, etc. No fuel . . . but it would do your heart good to be in our tent, to hear our songs and the cheery conversation."

Doesn't that dauntless spirit—facing some momentous challenge and facing it fearlessly—move and stir you? Doesn't every heart and mind know that that is the mark of a real master of life? Few would disagree with Cicero's remark: "Whoever is brave is a man of great soul."

But I find, as I look at my life and the years of counseling with people who come to me to discuss their difficulties and problems, that the fears that really erode us, that keep us on the down side rather than on top of life, are not those that come from such portentous situations. Rather, it is more insidious fears that haunt each hour. We may not know of them or we may try to hide them, but they are there all the time, lurking in the background every day.

Who among us is constantly weakened by the terror of cataclysmic events where life and death are ever in the balance? Few, I think—if any at all. But many of us are slaves to more subtle and debilitating fears: a permeating sense of inadequacy, a nagging fear of failing, of not measuring up to expectations; the disquieting sense of guilt, conscious or unconscious, with its fear of retribution, of being found out. Then there are pride and vanity, which we protect and try to cover up even from ourselves but which bring ever-continuous fears: of being rejected, of being unnoticed, of being thought unimportant. For many another it may be the fear of age, of being alone, or the fear of pain, or illness, or death. Whatever it may be, in whatever form it comes, it makes us cowards, rather than masters.

Katherine Mansfield confesses in her letters, "I believe the greatest failing of all is to be frightened. When I look back on my life all my mistakes have been made because I was afraid."

That failing, with the errors it prompts us to make, presents each man with some hobgoblin of fear.

Before we talk about ways of dealing with this problem, let me point out that there is a positive potential in the capacity to feel fear. The heightening of concern, the alertness, the keying up and the concentration of energy, that are released are to be expected, and can be productive.

Each Easter thousands of choirs and congregations in Christendom sing Handel's "Hallelujah Chorus." That great composition, from *The Messiah,* was written in a miraculously short twenty-odd days. At that time one side of Handel's body was paralyzed; his creditors were breathing down his neck; the threat of imprisonment was at his door; and fear hovered over the instrument where he was at work. But they served as spurs, making possible his prodigious and immortal effort. *The Messiah* might possibly never have been composed without that stimulus of alarm.

But whereas fear has its place on such occasions in life, where it may be a healthy prod to help us resist or speed up our reactions, without control and direction it can be a persisting, insidious destroyer.

It is interesting to note how fear seems to provide an extraordinary sense of well-being. You and I at times may even deliberately seek to expose ourselves to certain fearsome experiences. And we seem to derive physical exhilaration from them. I think this explains, at least in part, why individuals climb mountains or participate in hazardous automobile races or queue up in long lines before the roller coaster at amusement resorts. We may not even realize it, but the fact seems to be that such activities stimulate the whole endocrine system in the body and give us a sense of high physical, mental, and spiritual tone.

But fear can be perverted. Such an exhilaration can be disastrous if prolonged. Whereas normal fear may lead to efficiency and an extra output of energy, abnormal and persistent fear, buried within the personality, leads to complete inefficiency. Wisely controlled, fear prepares us to meet emergencies, providing an intelligent caution and sensitiveness needed to do any job well. But ungoverned anxieties and phobias (i.e., fears attached to objects that are not in themselves dangerous) are damaging, eating away at the health of body and soul. I believe psychologists, philosophers, and theologians agree that uncontrolled or repressed fear can poison the mind and weaken the whole character, paralyzing the will and shackling a free response to life.

Some years ago James L. McIntyre, lecturer in psychology in the University of Aberdeen, made a study of the history of fear. He considered the predominant fears of precivilized man: lightning and thunder and wild animals, with their immediacy and intensity. Turning to contemporary man and his problems, he affirmed that what modern fear has "lost in intensity and materiality it has gained in extensity, in persistence, in refinement of torture."

We will not argue with him. Living as we do under the awful threat of an international war that could in a few hours destroy the civilization that has taken centuries to build, we breathe the air of fear minute by minute. When we add to our burden, as so many of us do, the fear of being misunderstood, of being disliked, of being found out, of being hurt or rejected or lonely, of making decisions, we break down the protective devices for well-being.

How can we rid ourselves of these hobgoblins?

Individually, we can do more about it than we may suspect. First, though, it is necessary to get at the roots of our anxieties by careful, honest self-evaluation.

In the church where I am minister, each parishioner was sent a memento at a significant time in the history of the congregation. Reminiscent of the "Communion tokens" taken by elders of the Church of Scotland prior to the sacrament of the Holy Communion, the bronze memento sent to our people had on it a phrase from the Bible. In my judgment, it expresses one of the most provocative thoughts in the history of human ideas and spiritual adventure. It has only five words: "Let a man examine himself."

That sentence asks a man to turn inward some of the attention he pours on the outside. "Be honest with yourself," it says. "Examine your motives, your concerns, your fears, in your own quietude. You can be completely honest. You have only yourself in this consultation. You don't have to rationalize or try to hide anything. No one is listening but you. You don't have to strain to get someone else to understand." When sincerity and candor are present, such a self-examination can be healthful, curative.

I understand that many so-called "instinctive reactions" of animals can be traced to early experiences. Notice how that old cat jumps whenever a dog barks, even though the cause for fear is some distance away and the cat is completely safe from attack. The reason? As a little kitten it wasn't afraid of dogs. But once a dog barked and jumped at the kitten. It was a terrifying experience, and now that fear returns whenever a dog barks.

Our pussy cat is not able to let reason trace back to her early experience. She cannot come to the point where she can say, "This is a great folly I'm engaging in. A waste of effort."

But man can! I knew a man who was extremely sensitive and felt that he never was adequately appreciated in his work. He flitted from one job to another, always leaving with hurt feelings and bitterness. To others it appeared that his nose was always out of joint. Finally he did a bit of constructive self-examination and concluded that the drive to prove himself, the need to be appreciated, the fear of failing, went back to a misunderstanding of what his father had expected of him.

A man who had spent his life in supervising the personnel of a large corporation told me of an employee of his company who literally became "a new man." He had shown fine potentialities, and his superiors were interested in grooming him for a job with greater responsibility. But he was timid and seemed to constantly be holding back. He gave the impression of inner insecurity, even though his competence could be seen and was acknowledged by all his associates. My friend reported, "It took more than six months to try to help that man get to the source of his trouble. But he did. It was the result of having an overbearing father. As a lad, he couldn't please his father, and had let the frustrations of boyhood cause anxiety and trouble in his manhood."

That man, able to see, understand, and then laugh at his fear, gained a confidence and ease commensurate with his potentialities. He achieved high rank in the war and returned to his business to become one of its most able leaders.

A woman, outwardly inflexible and stern but inwardly troubled and tense, was able to trace, by self-examination, the source of her fear. Although she had tried to keep it locked tight inside, the cause of her trouble was guilt. A girlhood indiscretion had sapped away her best self for years, hobbling a happy adjustment to life. Fortunately, the perspective and wider understanding that comes with maturity finally permitted her to cleanse herself of this guilt and to find her way, which in earlier years seemed impossible.

We meet people we oppose. Why? What are the reasons that cause us to bristle, to be on edge, to feel anger or resentment? The answer is to be found in: "Let a man examine himself." Let reason, good judgment, honesty, and forgiveness cleanse our own soul before we judge other people. This is necessary for the conquest of fear and mastery of life.

If an individual, with complete honesty, will examine, for example, his need to dominate, to appear superior, he very likely will uncover a fear of being in a subordinate position. He may see that he is injuring his marriage, hurting the relationships with his children by continually trying to prove himself superior. That discovery of truth about himself will be hard to accept; it will be distressing. But it can never be damaging if it leads him from his little world of illusions to the world as it really is. Indeed, it can open the doors to humility and self-understanding and so lead to a more organized, masterful personality. As the neurologist, Abraham Myerson, said of this catharsis, "There is mental gain, character growth, as a result."

We consciously and unconsciously play tricks on ourselves. The fear of being hurt, the sense of envy or jealousy may be a natural part of our being, but an overweening fear of being hurt, of appearing weak or subordinate, can cause us to be completely dishonest with ourselves and with others. Often we will criticize the jealousy or envy or oversensitivity in other people, trying to pretend that we are not at fault ourselves. But as we develop the art of examining ourselves, we will transform the constructive power of fear into useful purpose. Any step we make in this direction, however faltering and small, is progress toward our goal, for as Lao-tse so wisely saw, "the journey of a thousand miles begins with one step."

Many of us have our fears abated and courage strengthened by association with people who are less fearful than ourselves.

Charles Darwin, in his *Naturalist's Voyage,* writes of observing sheep dogs in South America. He was intrigued by the fact that these dogs, when separated from the flocks, were extremely timid. But when with the sheep they were fearless and ferocious. His explanation was that the dogs, from birth, had been brought up with sheep. When they were with their own they had courage, but when alone they had none.

Man reacts in similar fashion. The timid individual can be buoyed up in the crowd and can present to the world a courage that is impossible to feel if he is alone. If we keep our fears to ourselves, trying to hide them from others and ourselves, we will never discover that our neighbors are probably facing similar problems and therefore have a sympathy and appreciation for our anxieties.

I was told about a woman who, years back, had let a really wasteful fear debilitate her strength. She had such terror of aging that she literally brought herself to the brink of a breakdown. But a neighbor with whom she shared her worries, together with a thoughtful and sensitive physician, were able to lead her to see, among other things, that she wasn't alone. Her fear, they showed her, was a widespread one. Through their experience and understanding they let her see, too, that real beauty is more than skin-deep. She rediscovered the truth that character, a growing wisdom, a capacity for humor, were more integral to charm and loveliness than cosmetics and face-lifting. But the most important thing she learned through and from her friends was that she was not alone.

Recently I read in a college magazine an article dealing with the anxieties of young people at that crucial stage in life. One of the intelligent observations the writer made was this, "One thing we must learn early; *sharing one's worries and fears with a trusted friend makes them tolerable.*" Then the counselor went on to say, "But pick the person or those persons carefully. Age is not all important. The important questions to ask are: Can he be counted on to keep your confidence? Can he be sympathetic without himself sharing your fear-ridden perspective? Does he really try to understand what life seems like to you?" People of all ages should remember this.

Janet Whitney has written of the visit made by Elizabeth Guerney Fry to a gloomy woman's yard at Newgate Prison on a cold January day in 1817.

The turnkeys on the outside were desperately afraid to enter the yard. They warned Elizabeth Fry that the women inside would scratch and claw at her and tear her clothes off.

With the quiet authority that comes from fearlessness she replied, "I am going in—and alone. I thank you for your kind intentions, but you are not to come with me." The turnkeys reluctantly opened the door and Elizabeth Fry passed through and walked among these women, who had been reduced to crime and filth and despair. Embittered and angered against life, they usually fought any and all who entered. But they did not do so now.

She talked to the prisoners about motherhood and asked them to tell her of the injustices they suffered. She began to light some lamps of hope as she talked with them of a subject they no longer discussed: the business of making plans for a better future. The writer, Janet Whitney, in describing Elizabeth Fry's departure, says, "She left behind her an inhabitant very strange to Newgate, one usually as much abandoned at its doors as at the very gate of hell, that revivifying spirit of human vitality called Hope."

We must try to offer hope to each other through contact and the sharing of human travail.

Association with others sometimes reveals that our fears are really picayune in comparison to the burdens that others have met and are shouldering. We can see in them the ability to go ahead, with a growing courage, *in spite of anxieties*. If others can do it, we can too!

It is reported that Edmund Burke once said, "Never despair, but if you do, work on in despair." There are many people who never really rid themselves of their fears or anxiety, but they have, as can we, a persistence that makes them stick to their guns in spite of all odds. Knowing them can help us to master our fate.

I shall always remember the influence of a friend who was involved in what might have been a serious highway accident. I drove by just as the accident occurred, and pulled up off the road in front of the damaged cars.

There was an electrifying fear in the atmosphere. Perhaps people were injured. Passing cars might crash into the damaged ones. Gasoline from the smashed vehicles ran over the traffic lanes. What if a lighted cigarette were thrown onto the road?

Among the individuals in the accident were several women and children and we could see the panic in their eyes and voices and tense bodies. But my friend, who had been driving one of the cars involved, walked slowly, spoke quietly. By no gesture did he add to anyone's anxiety. Rather the contrary.

Later I asked him how he had managed to present such quiet and calm front. His response was, "What is, *is!* I have nurtured in my mind for years the idea of Jesus that we don't grow an inch by anxiety. That thought was with me during the accident. It's with me now." With such courage, peace, resolution, we can handle any situation and teach others to do so.

In the dark days of February, 1942, Lord Beaverbrook quoted to Mr. Winston Churchill from a speech recorded in the writings of Thucydides: "Open no more negotiations with Sparta. Show them plainly that you are not crushed by your present affliction. They who face calamity without wincing, and who offer the most energetic resistance, these, be they states or individuals, are the truest heroes." That statement, made centuries before, imparted stanch resolution to Englishmen in the 20th century A.D. Wherever there is contact with constructive self-mastery, there always is constructive power.

One of the reasons the Church persists is that we are strengthened just in our coming together. We come, on the Sabbath day, each of us faulty, subject to terror and temptation. None of us is able to stand up and say, "I'm perfect." Quite the opposite. We are there, needing, seeking, some higher level of peace within ourselves, with our fellows, and with eternity. We can't sing together or try to pray together and know each other without a comfort and an assurance and a quieting of our anxieties. The ultimate source of these is in a growing understanding of and faith in God. As Epictetus, the philosopher who was a slave, said: "I am content with that which happens; for I think that what God chooses is better than what I choose."

This philosophy is founded on a conviction that the heart of creation has more knowledge of the ordering of life than any individual can ever have.

In my judgment one of the ways that we, like Epictetus, can achieve this freedom from the bondage of fear is by a deepening understanding of the nature of God, which reveals His compassion, good will, love; and inspires us to trust, have courage, be kind. To grow in this faith is to let more and more of love into our thinking, into our being, and free ourselves of the shackles of anxiety. The Bible puts it truly, "There is no fear in love, but perfect love casteth out fear."

I think that we can and should do so much more in the way of developing a deep good will as we face the conflict in the international scene today. So many of the chasms between the East and the West exist because of fear, which in turn produces faulty actions in relationships and negotiations. One of the most constructive ways we can and must make progress is through a change of attitude, a change of conviction, growing out of the knowledge that we are all a part of one human family. We must all find the faith that the world and all our lives are subject to a Providence which will claim all things in eternity. Each of us must say, "I will fear no evil," not because of my little achievements on the road to self-mastery, nor because of the support and insight gained from my fellow men, helpful as they have been. "I will fear no evil" says the exalted 23rd Psalm, *"for thou art with me."* This faith will sweeten and clear the waters of life.

Recently, in restudying the first chapter of Genesis, I was struck anew by the nobility of that epic concept of creation, which exultantly proclaims, "In the beginning God created the heavens and the earth."

One idea particularly touched me with its vitality. As the crown of His creative work, God made man in His own image. Man, as the highest and final order of the creative process, was made lord over all creation, over the creatures that flew in the air, the fish that swam in the sea, the creeping things and animals that inhabited the earth, the trees and grasses and herbs. He was not created to be a slave. He was to be God's regent here on the earth, to walk with a confident and kingly tread. We should never forget God's intent for us to let it dwell deep in our consciousness, giving us a surer sense that life has meaning, that we have a purpose.

In the growth of such a conviction we will begin to feel a harmony with all of creation, with all that happens. In time, possessing an invincible power, we shall overcome and cast out all fear.

VII

MEASURING UP
TO THE STANDARD
OF GOODNESS

O give thanks unto the Lord; for he is good: because his mercy endureth forever.

Psalms 118:1

... do good to them that hate you ... That ye may be children of your Father which is in heaven: for he maketh his sun to rise on the evil and on the good.

Matthew 5:44, 45

Goodness I call the habit, and the goodness of nature the inclination. This of all the virtues and dignities of the mind, is the greatest, ... without it man is a busy, mischievous, wretched thing.

Francis Bacon

Heaven prepares good men with crosses; but no ill can happen to a good man.

Ben Jonson

A real man is he whose goodness is a part of himself.

Mencius

Good, the more communicated, the more abundant grows.

Milton

Doing good is the only certainly happy action of a man's life.

Sir P. Sidney

> Howe'er it be, it seems to me,
> 'Tis only noble to be good,
> Kind hearts are more than coronets,
> And simple faith than Norman blood.

Tennyson

Real goodness does not attach itself merely to this life; it points to another world.

Daniel Webster

Iɴ *East of Eden*, John Steinbeck writes, "I be-lieve that there is one story in the world and only one . . . Human beings are caught—in their lives, in their hungers and ambitions, in their avarice and cruelty, and in their kind-ness and generosity too—in a net of good and evil. . . . A man, after he has brushed off the dust and chips of his life, will have left only the hard, clean question: was it good or was it evil? Have I done well, or ill?

"We have only one story. All novels, all poetry, are built on the never-ending contest in ourselves of good and evil. And it occurs to me that evil must constantly respawn, while good, while virtue, is immortal. Vice has always a new fresh young face, while virtue is venerable as nothing else in the world is."

Indeed, there is continuing power to goodness. I've never been able to completely agree with Shakespeare in his con-tention that "The evil that men do lives after them; the good is oft interred with their bones." The reverse, I find, is just as likely true. How often, in talking, individuals speak of some act of goodness that occurred years before. Its influence went deep, still shining recollection.

Remember the story of the lion that never forgot the man who removed a thorn from his paw and years later spared his life in the arena? So do acts of goodness imprint them-selves and live on within us, sometimes coming to our rescue years later.

The word "good" in Anglo-Saxon and Old Saxon was spelled g-o-d. Obviously, the relationship between "good" and "God" is very close, for in goodness there is a quality of divinity. In his search to know the nature of God, man long ago discovered the truth when he vowed, "God is good . . . His mercy endureth forever."

Little wonder is it that some of the most noble masters of life have been the men who have expressed or done the greatest good. Said Demosthenes, "Everything great is not always good, but all good things are great." Think of the individuals in the long sweep of history—and those we have known in the briefer limits of our own personal lives—who have succeeded most in living worthwhile lives. Have they not measured very high against the standard of goodness?

A woman who came to me some time ago is typical, I believe, of all of us. After she had outlined the troubling and unhappy experiences that had beaten her down, I said to her, "We've covered rather fully the negative and disturbing things that have happened to you. Before we have our next meeting, I'd like you to make a list of the people you've known who have done you not the worst—which we've talked about today—but the best."

When I saw her a week later her attitude had changed; there was a note of self-confidence that hadn't been there before. She began to tell me first of a playmate when she was a little girl of four who had given her a doll in a gesture of love and admiration. Then there was a wonderful aunt and a sensitive teacher who had encouraged her through the adolescent years with their confidence in her. Next came an old handy man and a wise clergyman who had given her an unexpected hand of guidance when the road became especially rough.

"There have been so many good people I've known," she said as she left, "I'm so glad to have dug them out of memory.

There's no better way of putting it than to say *I've let them live again. And for me they make life worth living once more.*"

In the Apostle Paul's second letter to Timothy are the words, "And if a man also strives for mastery, yet is he not crowned except he strive lawfully." In Paul's thinking the law was good. It was identified with order, consideration, fair play, justice. We can paraphrase his thought, without doing him an injustice, to have it read, "If a man strives for high achievement in life, he will truly be crowned if he follows the path of goodness."

In an extended journey across India of some months ago, I felt the profoundly good influence of Gandhi on that land and people. In the north, at New Delhi, where his body was cremated, rich and poor came to do him homage, and with them I, too, bowed in silent recognition of his greatness. Weeks later, at the very southern tip of India, where the Indian Ocean, the Arabian Sea, and the Bay of Bengal mingle their waters, I again mused on his life. Gandhi's ashes had been scattered on those waves, which, in time, must ripple out and touch the shores of all nations.

Before I addressed an audience in the city of Madurai, toward the end of my stay in India, I stood outside the auditorium, where a statue of Gandhi had been erected; and I read the inscription at its base: "There is no religion higher than truth and righteousness." Here was expressed what I had felt increasingly throughout the length and breadth of that vast subcontinent. Gandhi was a great man because he expressed in thought and action the qualities of goodness. His religion *was* that of truth and righteousness. In his life was the merging power of mercy and compassion, and his own words reveal the strength of his convictions. They show, too, the foundation on which his character was built.

He wrote, ". . . love is the basis of the search for truth . . .

I am realizing every day that the search for truth is vain unless it is founded on love. It is quite proper to resist and attack a system, but to resist and attack its author is tantamount to resisting and attacking oneself. For we are all subject to the same weakness and are children of one and the same Father; and as such the divine powers within us are infinite. To injure a single human being is to injure those divine powers within us, and thus the harm reaches not only that one human being, but with him the whole world."

Indeed, a man who thought and wrote like that lived by truth and love, by humanity.

Our relatively new science of psychology is helpful in enabling us to see more clearly the closely woven threads of good and evil. The older science of theology teaches that evil is fallen or unregenerated good. Psychology has pointed out that there is no instinct, no primary impulse in man that has not contributed to the development of the race. We may say that conceit or avarice appear as wrong, but psychological studies show that these wrongs are perversions of instincts that in purer form can be of benefit to mankind. Evil is the misplacement of a necessary and basic good impulse. As J. Arthur Hadfield, the English psychotherapist, expresses it, a primary impulse is misplaced if it persists beyond its phase, if it is directed to wrong ends, or if it is attached to wrong objects.

The charitable and forgiving spirit in the right place, directed to the right end and the right object is magnificent. In the story of David there is an instance when, after being unjustly treated by King Saul, he had to flee for his life, and with a few loyal followers he hid in an isolated cave. Saul came into the region with his warriors, intent on finding and destroying David. In his search Saul entered the very cave where David and his men were hidden. Wearied, the King lay down and fell asleep. David's followers urged him to kill Saul. Here was a perfect opportunity to be rid of his enemy.

Instead of plunging a dagger in Saul's heart, David quietly cut a portion of cloth from his oppressor's mantle. Later he showed it to Saul, thereby indicating that he might have taken the King's life but had spared him.

Where in all literature is there a more noble example of charitable forgiveness than Jesus? Hanging on the cross in an agony of pain, having cause for bitterness toward fate and those who were torturing Him, He yet petitioned, "Father, forgive them, they know not what they do."

But a charitable disposition toward one's fellow men in some circumstances may be the opposite of good. The weakened individuals walking this earth who have been pampered and coddled and sheltered by overly solicitous and forgiving parents are victims of an intended good gone beyond its place. Such kindliness does more harm than good. The violent reaction against such misplaced good will cause the cry: "Damn your charity, give me justice."

Granting that Steinbeck is right in saying that the only drama is that of men and women caught in a net of good and evil, how do we, in the net, achieve more good than evil? By what means do we leave an imprint for good rather than for evil on the orbit of life? The first and the last thing I know is that there needs to be a continual cultivation of good ideas. We grow in goodness as we think good thoughts, do good deeds, associate with good people, and search for goodness of spirit all our days.

The Bible tells of a man named Joseph of Aramathea who, when there was no place to lay the lifeless and broken body of Christ, gave his own tomb. Other than that act, the only description we have of the man is this: "And, behold, there was a man named Joseph, a counsellor; and he was a good man, and a just." I am sure that there is more than that one act by which he achieved immortality; there must have been a day-by-day pattern of goodness that increased as his spirit and his thought drew closer to God.

I've had limited experience in gardening, but in my few attempts I have noticed that, in order for healthy plants to get a good start, it is necessary to cultivate them regularly. The weeds have to be systematically pulled out. But once the plants have a strong start, be they beans or tomatoes or what-have-you, the shade they create and their increasing stature are a means of thwarting the weedy growth that would diminish their healthy life. The plants themselves suffocate the destructive elements. Cultivating is still necessary, but with each hoeing they achieve greater strength and health.

Some time back I was speaking with a friend about the matter of continually feeding one's mind and spirit with sound and invigorating ideas. She responded by telling me of a method that worked for her. At the beginning of each day she sought through prayer to feel what she called "the vital vibrations" of her life in harmony with God. "If my creative energy can be placed in keeping with that which is eternally good," she said, "then the negative, the evil, the nonproductive and destructive thoughts and actions are eliminated. They simply die of starvation. But," she added, "I have to work at it all the time." Knowing that woman for years, I saw how her efforts paid off. The goodness she put into herself bore fruit in a good life.

I recall a man who had been an admirer of Emmet Fox and who had attended his lectures. He reported that Dr. Fox advocated time and time again "visiting" each day with God. No matter what it was called—a moment of meditation or prayer or anything else—let there be a regular time when one's soul opened to "the waters" of eternity. The stagnant pools of negativism, discouragement, bitterness, would be purified as the vast cleansing of the "living ocean" passed over them.

In whatever way we can best suit our own lives, we should use this technique for growth in goodness; faithfully begin each new stretch of time, each fresh task, with God; silently say, "My life, this world of which I am a part, my work, all are filled with good and potentiality. It was all made by God, who looked on it all and declared it was good. As I think and speak and act this day, I will only think and speak and act in keeping with that which is good."

Daily, hundreds of thousands of people find strength by reading devotional and inspirational literature. Each individual must experiment to find the best way, to cultivate and nourish his conscious and subconscious being. Most of us need "a starter" of some kind. It can be just one inspiring thought, one provocative idea, one beautiful line of poetry or one constructive phrase. For centuries men and women have found the Bible the inexhaustible source for such inspiration and guidance. Read it until, like Coleridge, you can say, "It finds me." Or muse over it until, as others put it, "I find marching orders for the day." Whatever your "starter," savor it. Apply it to yourself. In the visualization of the day ahead say to yourself "I will not be thrown by any setback or opposition. I may not avoid being knocked down. But it will be only for a moment."

Not long ago I was in the home of a man I had long admired. His services and achievements in our nation and abroad had been recognized through three generations. He was a man of integrity and dependability, a good man. In his eightieth year, he was just recovering from a serious illness. His wife took from the little table at the side of his chair an old Bible. The cover was worn with much handling and cracked with age. Throughout the book pages were marked dates written in pencil. Some were of the nineteenth century.

"At the age of nineteen my husband went on his first business trip to the Orient. This Bible went with him then and on many subsequent trips around the world." With love and admiration, as she looked at him, his wife added, "And when things were hard and temptations perhaps strong, he would put down the date of the reading of a chapter that had helped him over the hump." As I looked at that man I saw a great and good life. As I looked at the old Bible, placed in my hands, I know I was looking at the source of that greatness and goodness.

We begin to see the goodness of life, and become better ourselves from the seeing, as we respond constructively and positively to every situation.

Tolstoi, in *Anna Karenina,* speaks of the quiet and constant light that is seen on the faces of those who are successful. Of this I am sure: If we will put on our faces the quiet and steady light that looks at every situation, every event, every contact with another human being, with the idea that everything has good propensities and possibilities, we will find that it is so. We will see that life is good. The glow of that knowledge will be real.

A cheerful temperament, a dominant, positive mood will help us find the good life. Brahms found it. He thought well of everybody. He let children ride on him piggyback; delighted to listen to and lustily applaud the gypsies who played at the fairs. There was a wonderful quality emanating from him in every situation, and individuals touched by that emanation reflected back the same quality.

Both Jews and Christians do a great injustice to their heritage when they force their religion into a dour, repressed, negative form of expression. Alexander Miller, in his book, *The Renewal of Man,* sensitively crystallized the outlook of the ancient Hebrew. He described it as, "A lip-smacking, exuberant delight in the ingenious beauty and variety of the created world; in wine and milk, olive-oil and honey. It is a world whose paths drop fatness, where the little hills rejoice on every side. Such a world," went on Mr. Miller, "has a place for heroism, but none for aestheticism."

One of the dominant traits of Jesus was just such a positive delight with all of life. Farmers and publicans, herdsmen and soldiers, holy men and sinners, lepers and fishermen—all found Him responsive. A biographer might be inclined to write only of His defeats. His disciples failed to understand Him. One was a traitor. The crowds that once hailed Him as Messiah demanded His crucifixion. Having lived in poverty, he died ignominiously on the cross. But such a plot would miss completely the power of Jesus. He was never defeated. His death became one of mankind's most stirring symbols of triumph. And the reason? The indestructible faith He had in life, in God and man. He gave that faith to others too. The biographer, to truly catch His spirit, must conclude with His own radiantly affirmative words, "My joy no man taketh from me."

We grow in goodness of character and the good life when we are willing to take the time and pay the price to find the good in even the worst situation.

Some time ago I was talking to one of the most successful men of our day. In the course of our conversation he made the statement that the best things that had come to his life had come out of what, on the surface, had always appeared to be the worst situations. Intrigued, I asked him to explain what he meant. He told me of his being fired from a position early in his career, but that crushing experience gave him the humility and sensitiveness and determination to be better. They proved to be tremendous assets when he started another job.

He told me of a bitter misunderstanding and of unjust claims made against him by a man he had trusted and had considered a friend. Business reverses at a later stage in his career were another setback. Out of every one of the occasions when he seemed to have been beaten down, he discovered positive values that enabled him to stand straighter than ever before.

He had something of the quality of Jacob when he came to the brook whose crossing would mark his return to his native land. All night long he wrestled with an unknown assailant. He was injured in the struggle. All his life he was to limp because of the encounter. Yet, as the dawn was breaking, he cried, "I will not let thee go except thou bless me." If we can say that to life, we can find the good in every difficult situation.

I am not advocating a Pollyanna attitude, which closes its eyes or glosses over difficulty or pain or sorrow or conflict. Rather, it's just the reverse. Take off the colored glasses; look at and grapple with your assailant openly, honestly, realistically. Wrestle with it until it is transmuted into something positive. And remember, one of the greatest and most powerful texts in the Bible is: "All things work together for good to them that love God."

To achieve self-mastery we must face up to our fluctuating moods and try to prevent sharp changes of attitude. They can be caused by physical weariness or physiological deficiencies. They can be brought on by overexertion, too much pressure on our nervous and mental resources. When the clouds of depression start gathering, we must do something constructive to dispel them. The mind that can contemplate goodness will be prepared for such emergencies and provide some safety value for the occasion.

For one person it may be a notebook, built up across the years, of ideas and quotations that have been helpful in his life. For another it may be a refreshing walk or an interlude of listening to music. One woman told of a method she uses, which apparently never fails her: "The floor of my laundry room always needs a cleaning. I keep putting it off. When I start getting blue, I make myself go to work scrubbing it up. When it's done I have a good feeling inside. I admire the shiny floor and tell myself that, if I can make myself do that, there's nothing at all that can lick me." Often some task requiring physical exertion lifts low spirits and sends a bad mood packing.

Knowing when we need a letting up or a letting down would save many of us from working halfheartedly, and irritating ourselves and others. One doctor I know says, "When I get at a low ebb, I do my patients more good by going away on a fishing trip than I could possibly do them by barking at them in my office."

In the Book of Proverbs is a beautiful description of a worthy woman who was highly honored by her husband. The chapter describes her as doing him "good and not evil all the days of her life." The source of her goodness is probably explained by her many-faceted interests in life. She was a seamstress, a planner and organizer. She was interested in business and conservation; she cultivated her own character and philosophy and disposition. She was interested in people. Her horizons were broad, and consideration flowed from her to the poor and needy. This variety and change of pace surely made it possible for her to achieve the resourcefulness to master the bad moods that might otherwise have downed her.

I'm inclined to believe that most men and women cultivate varied interests. If one activity won't turn back the clouds of despair, there are others that will. If the children are on edge and discouraging, there's always one's coin collection to re-examine, or the piano to which one can turn for relaxation.

I have always liked the analogy of the little ship that bobs along on the vast and rolling sea. Water is all around it, unknown depths are beneath it. But all the water of the world cannot sink that little ship *unless it gets on the inside.*

And so it is with our mental attitudes, our spiritual fortifications. Believing in goodness in the world, having the conviction that our lives are made for good living and good action, we can build the framework of a seaworthy ship of life. And then all the turbulent water through which we may pass can do us no harm because we are prepared and protected—we will not let it get on the inside.

We should touch on the matter of the seemingly undesirable things that could happen to us which cause us trouble and trembling at the very thought of them. There is death. There is the thought of being handicapped. There is the possibility that the individual to whom our life is most deeply tied may be taken from us. Such events, as we envision them, are certainly not good.

No good, happy life—none that is free—is lived with such a sword always hanging over it, casting its ominous shadow on the present moment. Neither is there satisfaction in never facing these matters at all. They must be dealt with, and then be done with.

There are many ways that man has sought and applied, with varying degrees of success, to be rid of the sense of doom. Since it should not be totally excluded from consciousness, or ignored, only the positive approaches can be considered. Think of the sad and ominous possibilities as tares that grow amid the good grain. Looking at life this way, man can say to himself, "If I must encounter you, I will do so without defeat. I will take more from you than you will take from me." Such admirable spirit was revealed by a woman of refinement and privilege who said, "If worse comes to the worst, I shall still be needed. There will be a place for me. There will always be something I can do. At the very least, I can minister to the sick in hospitals."

But for larger numbers of people there has been a surer way, tested and tried across the centuries. It is to live with the great thought that man need fear no evil for God is with him. This is the ultimate way to win victory over the possibility of evil. It may be helpful to think of perfect good when we use the word "God." There is nothing that can overcome us if we say, in our hearts and the deepest depths of our minds, "No evil can cause me consternation . . . for thou art with me."

The individual who lives by that conviction lives more and more the good life. More and more the masterful life becomes his.

VIII

MASTERING
THE YES AND NO
DEPARTMENT

But let your communication be, Yea, yea; Nay, nay; for whatsoever is more than these cometh of evil.

Matthew 5:37

Be not either a man of many words; or busy about too many things.

Marcus Aurelius

Firmness, both in sufferance and exertion, is a character which I would wish to possess. I have always despised the whining yelp of complaint and the cowardly, feeble resolve.

Robert Burns

Take time to deliberate; but when the time for action arrives, stop thinking and go in.

Andrew Jackson

Decide not rashly. The decision made
Can never be recalled. The Gods implore not,
Plead not, solicit not; they only offer
Choice and occasion, which once being passed
Return no more.

Longfellow

Once to every man and nation comes the moment to decide,
In the strife of Truth with Falsehood, for the good or evil side.

Lowell

Here I stand; I can do no otherwise. God help me. Amen.

Martin Luther

Men must decide on what they will not do, and then they are able to act with vigor in what they ought to do.

Mencius

There is no mistake; there has been no mistake; and there shall be no mistake.

The Duke of Wellington

In 1932 the famous cartoonist, David Low, produced a drawing that became one of the most widely circulated cartoons in the world. This was not just because its message was particularly timely; it was tinged with eternal truth too.

A little boat labeled "World Money Problem" was seen rocking amid giant waves that towered over and all around it. In one end several people were feverishly bailing out water. A vicious leak had the craft almost half-filled. Those busy individuals were labeled "Middle Europe." At the other end three figures representing America, England, and France were huddled together. Sitting on the sides of the boat, they were doing their best to stay dry, and looking with only a touch of concern at the busy bailers. The conversation of the three made the caption of the cartoon, which read: "Phew! That's a nasty leak. Thank goodness it's not at our end of the boat."

The folly of that attitude can be seen by a first grader. The leak in the boat is everybody's business who is aboard. Surely there isn't any masterful dealing with life unless there is knowledge that all of us are involved with mankind. There must be more participation than withdrawal, more action than reaction, more moving forward than retreating backward.

The individuals who do respond, whatever the issue may be, on the side of justice, humanity, mercy, good will are automatically given the tribute of being a master of life. How often I have seen discussions and judgments and feelings gravitate around and settle about the man who has expressed himself with clarity on the side of justice. Alan Paton put it this way, "To stand up for the freedom of others is one of the marks of those who are free, just as to fail to do so is one of the marks of those who are ready to be enslaved." We instinctively sense that. All men react to it and are pulled toward it as bits of metal to a magnet.

A small religious paper occasionally comes my way from friends in Czechoslovakia. In the summer of 1957 an article described the anniversary ceremonies held in commemoration of the terrible destruction of the little village of Lidice. The paper reprinted a letter from Albert Schweitzer written to Professor Hromadka and all who had part in the solemn occasion. He said that it was important for us to remember the black inhumanity at Lidice because it might restrain mankind from repeating such a brutal orgy. Then he added: "We must take up the struggle against the ideas of inhumanity which we still suffer to exist among us. Humanism is the basis of civilization, and we must stand on its side."

I have been so imbued with the beauty of the King James version that I cannot refrain from citing: "Let your communication be, Yea, yea; Nay, nay; for whatsoever is more than these cometh of evil."

What Jesus meant was this: Let it be known where you stand and then stand there. Stop hedging. Avoid long and cloudy explanations. Don't make involved and impressive promises. Watch the business of swearing, crossing your heart, and taking oaths. Be of clear integrity. Let it be yes or no! And then stick to it.

One of the reasons that our personal and corporate life is often ineffectual is simply because we fail to take the Master's counsel. Liston Pope of Yale University has made many incisive criticisms of our times. In an address some time back he characterized us as being an era of conflicting affirmation and negation. We are, he said, living "Jekyll-and-Hyde lives in a schizoid world."

Let some basic questions be asked.

Do you believe in the United Nations? Likely the answer will be confusing: Yes—but no when it comes to merging with other nations some of our national sovereignty in the interests of world organization.

Are you committed to the principle of equality? Yes! But also no when it comes to certain of our minority groups.

What of the proposition that man is created for and capable of goodness? Are you for or against? Yes, I'm for it. But not when I see the chicanery and the selfishness in some men.

Are you at peace? Are you for peace in the world? And again our answer is a complex and an involved potpourri that comes out saying both yes and no.

Of course, there is wisdom and realism in seeing that there are infinite shades between the black and the white. But what Jesus tells us is this: "Let it be known what you're looking for. Let it be clear, when you do find the distinction, where you're going to stand, and finally when the paths open up, which way you will follow!"

It is also proper, in preparing for mastery in this area, to recognize the danger of ill-advised or quick judgments. Those who have often made fully formed and worthy contributions to life out of their own decisiveness and convictions have often been individuals of great capacity for thought and considered judgment. William of Orange, known as "The Silent One," was such a man. Thinking of him and similar individuals led Carlyle to exclaim, "In thy own mean perplexities, do thou thyself but *hold thy tongue for one day;* on the morrow, how much clearer are thy purposes and duties; what wreck and rubbish have those mute workmen within thee swept away." Giving consideration to an important matter is essential; but it is equal importance, at least, to come to a decision and take a firm stand. One can make evaluations too quickly on the one hand, and on the other wander too long in a fog of uncertainty.

I think it is important to also see that it is no great sin to change your position or modify your convictions, if you are led to a higher position or a sounder conviction. The wisdom that affirms, "Consistency is the hobgoblin of little minds," should comfort you if time and circumstance seem to demand a change of course. But here again the important thing is to set a course rather than merely drift. It is impossible to go in all directions at once, and disastrous to go in no direction at all.

There is merit in our seeing the value of definiteness, of decisiveness in the make-up and development of our own character as well as appreciating it in other people. On shipboard for the first time some years ago, I was impressed with the lifeboat drill. Prior to setting sail I had been reading of major catastrophes at sea. The awful sense of what might occur in a hurricane or a wreck at sea was upon me. During the lifeboat drill I was comforted by the definiteness of the arrangements for the passengers' safety. Had the instructions been merely casual statements that there were lifeboats on the ship and also adequate life preservers and rafts, I would have been quite nervous and anxious. But being informed as to the precise place and lifeboats the passengers were assigned to in the event of danger and receiving instructions about the location of life jackets provided a sense of security and order.

We who are parents constantly see the need for preciseness, for definiteness, for clarity of thought, in the rearing of our children. It is by showing them choices in precise rules for conduct, by stimulating their own development in the yes and no department, that their outward and inner security develops.

A friend of mine, recounting his schooling during boyhood and young adulthood, recalled one fourth-grade teacher who stood out above all the rest. "There was no nonsense about her. She was definite. You always knew where you stood. If you did mediocre work, she let you know it and know it promptly." He went on to tell how that woman's influence was one of the major ones in his whole life. The setting up of standards, the clear-cut requirements, the definite expectations which she put before him and the other pupils were powerful factors in building character.

But we can surely add, when we consider this business of decisiveness for us moderns, that we all need help because we are pulled in so many different directions. We are like the three-year-old with her mask and Hallowe'en costume on who looked at herself in the mirror and exclaimed, "Mommy, I don't know which is me." Many claims are put on us as citizens, as parents, as church members, as participants in a profession or a business. We are always facing situations where it is so hard to know whether to say yes or no. Questions constantly plague us: Is it a time to make a change? Should I modify my point of view or should I retain what I've gone by so far? In this particular situation shall I speak or shall I keep quiet? How will I serve the highest purpose in the involved situation I now face, by discretion or boldness? How can I keep the weights of social responsibility and the filling of my personal needs in a wholesome and intelligent balance?

Another cartoonist, Robert Osborn, in a recent publication, *Osborn on Leisure,* portrays all too vividly the pressured dilemmas of modern man. One sketch shows the modern housewife, like a puppet, with strings attached at every joint and extremity, including her nose. She is being pulled in all directions. She, as does her male counterpart, needs guidance on the question of what to hold on to and what to let go.

But you wouldn't expect me, and I would be a fool to attempt, to give you some detailed blueprint that would propose to fit the situation of each individual. Each of us must work out our own destiny in terms of our particular abilities, inclinations, temperaments. The balancing of the scales between yeas and nays will differ for every person; but we must have that balance.

Stephen F. Bayne, Jr., Episcopal Bishop of Olympia, in an excellent speech some time ago stated, "All true teaching aims to teach mankind how to take sides." Some people shy off from revealing where they stand because they claim they may hurt someone else's feelings. That is a point to be considered. Tolerance, sympathy, and appreciation for the feelings and opinions of others are certainly important factors. Since people can feel a sense of rejection if we too vigorously or violently express our viewpoint and seemingly denounce, exclude, or condemn theirs, special attention should be given to our spirit and attitude as we take our stand.

It has been my observation that if sensitivity and consideration are present, there is no position that cannot be taken with dignity. And taken or given in that spirit, any stand can earn the respect of even those who may seem most opposed to it. One of the most enriching qualities of conversation and human contact comes out of differing points of view. Contrariwise, one of the most deadening experiences in life is participation in a group where there is a lack of decisiveness. Man needs the vitality, life, strength that comes when he can say "Yes" or "No" and mean it.

And certainly this is the way to growth. Self-mastery depends on being able to get off the fence and make decisions, whether they are of a personal nature or have social, political, or business implications.

Some of us overextend ourselves because we don't know how to say "No," when in reality there is more merit in being able to say "No" at the right time. We should be able to make that distinction and put it to best advantage.

An able business leader, who is of valuable service not only to his particular field but to the civic interests of this country and the world, once told me that from time to time he requested his secretary to bring in a little typewritten card for him to read at the beginning of the day. It had these words on it: "Have you asked God to help you keep your big mouth shut today?"

There is whimsy and charm in that question, and there is wisdom in knowing that one doesn't have strength unless it is conserved. A channeling of our capabilities is necessary in order to achieve our best. And one way to do so is to curtail our energy, expend it on the right things, and say a simple "No" to distracting claims and demands.

Olgivanna Lloyd Wright, in her book, *The Struggle Within,* has a suggestion for maintaining a healthy balance in our busy modern age: "When we find ourselves caught in this rush from one duty to another, we can well remember the enervating state that this very experience caused us in the past. Remembering this, we induce complete inner relaxation, during which time our poise is regained. We then evaluate calmly what we have been doing. In full consciousness we can leave it at that point, reassuring ourselves that in a more measured tempo at the proper time, we will again attend to our duties without destroying ourselves in fulfilling them. It is significant to learn how to make these conscious pauses."

A technique such as this, adapted to our own lives, may give us the wisdom to see and the strength to say no to unnecessary and unworthy expenditures of time and effort.

England's fine literary figure and politician-essayist, Thomas Macaulay must have been a rarely gifted man. If you read his biography you will learn that before he was eight years old he had written a *Compendium of Universal*

History. His mark as a literary figure was set high with the publication of an essay on Milton which appeared in the *Edinburgh Review.* Led to enter politics, he was elected to the House of Commons and made his first major speech for a most humane cause: removing the restrictions against Jews in England. Portions of the speech, said Sir Robert Peel, "were as beautiful as anything I have heard or read." Peel was saying what was on everyone's lips.

One essay and Macaulay was a towering figure in the literary world. One speech and all London was singing his praises as an orator. Appeals flooded in to write and speak on other topics, to champion other causes. But Macaulay was silent for a long time. Said Elbert Hubbard of him, "He practised self-restraint and knew better than to dilute his fame by holding argument with small men on little topics."

Self-restraint and self-mastery require that we say "No" to self-indulgence. "Strait is the gate and narrow is the way that leadeth unto life." If we decide that a complacent, a pleasure-seeking life is not what we want, we must deal sternly with the elements that complicate our life and drain and disperse our resources.

But what of our "Yes"? Are there any guides here? There are some suggested ones. The most obvious one, of course, is that, within the limits of our physical and psychic ability and our personal responsibilities, we can't go wrong in saying "Yes" to any opportunity to perform a real service to mankind.

One of the most provocative and one of the truest things ever said is: *"He that is greatest among you shall be servant of all."* This seems a total paradox, running in opposition to our deep and tenacious instincts. But it is true, says Jesus, and the truth of history is on His side, affirming that you and I and anybody else hasn't a chance in a billion of being remembered and thought worth while after a century has passed unless we try to do something in the category of "servants of all."

We should say "Yes" to a vision of life that pushes out beyond the horizon of just making a living for ourselves and providing material comforts for our families.

Frederick William Farr wrote of Marcus Aurelius that he was "the undisputed lord of the Roman world. He was seated on the dizziest and most splendid eminence which is possible for human grandeur to obtain. But this imperial elevation kindled no glow or pride or self-satisfaction in his meek and chastened nature. He regarded himself as being in fact the servant of all."

Say "Yes" to any purpose, any cause, that would enrich and serve mankind.

To perform life's tasks, we must constantly replenish our reservoirs of inner strength in order to maintain a steady flow of power. But if, in the performance of our duty, we completely exhaust ourselves and become drained and empty, we won't be able to meet our responsibilities. Therefore, we must learn how to say "Yes" to our duties, while saying "No" to oversolicitude in fulfilling them.

That was the fault of Martha in the New Testament. Hers was the duty of fixing the evening meal. To it she said, "Yea." But she poured herself too exhaustively into her duty, thereby missing one of the sweetest opportunities of being fed spiritually by the Master.

In too much single-mindedness there is destruction to the self. What does it profit a man if he piles up victories won, duties fulfilled, but has a vacuum where his soul should be?

Say "Yes" to the practice of doing one thing at a time. To procrastinate, to say "Yes and no, but I'll do it later," places great strain on our abilities and energies. It makes what could be done today an increasingly heavy burden for tomorrow, and often poisons a sense of accomplishment with a feeling of guilt.

Our life is always crowded, and we only add to the confusion when everything we have to do or could do is opened like a mail sack and dumped, willy-nilly, on the table. Said Goethe to Jane Carlyle during a very troubled period for her: "Do the thing at hand and the next will reveal itself in due course." There is a natural order to things if we will but proceed step by step in doing them.

Last but not least, we make no mistake in saying "Yes" to a growing faith that this is God's world, that we are His children, and that there is a purpose in life. Then add to that purpose the determination to do what we believe is God's will.

Edwin Markham in one of his poems wrote these words as coming from God Himself:

> I will leave man to make the fateful guess,
> Will leave him torn between the No and Yes;
> Leave him in tragic loneliness to choose,
> With all in life to win and all to lose.

Is that true? Up to a certain point, yes. But there's another facet to man's dilemma of choosing. In the Scriptures it is written: "I will not leave you alone. I will come unto you." And Jesus said, "Lo, I am with you always, even unto the end." In making fateful yes-and-no decisions, we become acquainted with one of the most profound experiences in life: namely, that the God who made us is with us.

The Bible counsels us, as we face life, to choose "whatsoever things are true, whatsoever things are honest, whatsoever things are just, whatsoever things are pure, whatsoever things are lovely, whatsoever things are of good report . . ." If we follow this advice, we will feel the Eternal Providence that inspired those words; His guidance will not lead us astray.

IX

MASTERY
FROM THE MYSTERY
OF INTUITION

. . . it was revealed to him [Simeon] by the Holy Ghost, that he should not see death, before he had seen the Lord's Christ.

Luke 2:26

This, therefore, is a law not found in books, but written on the fleshly tablets of the heart, which we have not learned from man, received or read, but which we have caught up from Nature herself, sucked in and imbibed; the knowledge of which we were not taught, but for which we were made; we received it not by education, but by intuition.

Cicero

The aims and ideals that move us are generated through imagination, but they are not made out of imaginary stuff. They are made out of the hard stuff of the world of physical and social experience. The new vision emerges through seeing old things in new relations serving a new end which the new end aids in creating.

John Dewey

. . . a kind of enthusiasm or extraordinary emotion of the soul . . .

Dryden

Intuition is the clear conception of the whole at once. It seldom belongs to man to say without presumption, "I came, I saw, I conquered.

Johann Kaspar Lavater

Imagination is controlling and using the energy of which we are made. Those who succeed in this have access, through their partial energy, to all energy. The thoughts of these men have the divinity of all energy: they do not die.

John Masefield

An ELDERLY WOMAN was telling of her town's favorite son. He was the home-town boy who went off into the wide world and made good. Said the aged lady, who had known the man from birth on, "When he was about fourteen years old, most folks, if asked where he was going to end up, would have said, 'The penitentiary.'

"He was the most harum-scarum boy in the neighborhood. If the Sunday school was disrupted, he was the one who was behind it. He graduated from college by the skin of his teeth." Then she smiled, "But I always knew he had mighty good stuff in him and one day we'd all be proud of him."

That woman had what we call an intuitive knowledge, or assurance, or faith. She "looked upon" that boy and came up with an evaluation altogether different from that which obvious facts and reasoned thought seemed to suggest. That's what intuition is. It's a source of knowledge that is based on an immediate comprehension of some truth. Intuitionalism opposes the idea that all of our knowledge or understanding or wisdom is based on observable facts, reasoned judgment, or intellectual processes.

Its examples are as legion as they are varied in our daily life. If you play golf, more than once you have heard a player say, "I just knew I was going to flub that drive," or, "I sensed the minute I started my back swing that the ball would end up in the pond."

A friend to whom I made this observation replied, "Yes,

it's sad but true. However, isn't the reverse also true? Can't the ball be visualized sailing straight down the fairway? And occasionally—very occasionally perhaps—doesn't it work that way? Please say it does, because I'd like to improve my score."

I assured him that it was true, and presented no bill for the secret. For I have often heard a player say when a game is over, "I can't explain it fully, but I was as sure as the sun is in the sky that I'd play well today. I felt right. I knew I'd win."

But look at other illustrations. Haven't you ever had the sense of some impending unpleasantness? Haven't you heard, in family discussions, someone say, "I knew the minute I got up this morning it was going to be a tough day, and it certainly worked out that way." Or, "I just felt it in my bones that that romance wouldn't last." Or someone says, "The moment I met that man, I knew immediately he'd fit into our organization," or, "I had the strangest sensation that that man couldn't be trusted." And someone else says, "The moment I saw that girl, I knew she was the one for me." So we express intuitive judgments about experiences and relationships with our fellow men.

This ability in man has a deeper and more significant aspect. It is not a mere tiddlywinks game of casual significance. Intuition, has also played a powerful part in scientific, aesthetic, moral, and religious discoveries.

One of the great spiritual insights was made by Plato, who affirmed, toward the end of his life, that the divine element was not coercive but persuasive. That thought came not from piling fact on top of fact, not from some process of logic. It was an inspiration of the mind, an illumination of the soul. It was what the philosopher Spinoza described as a form of knowledge that transcends that which is given by reason and is arrived at by the apprehension of the essence of things. Observation, evaluation, deduction, had their place, but Plato grasped or was given that insight in a flash of intuition.

If you want technical language for this endowment, you can put down the big word "cosmaesthesia." Cosmaesthesia is the feeling we are all endowed with for the relationship of things. It is the intuitive understanding of what's good for us and a sense of what's bad for us. You and I have a perception of what will contribute to our well-being. Those who have sought to analyze and describe this perception affirm that there is the feeling of the consequences of a reaction. That awareness of the factors that will determine a particular conclusion is called, in case you are interested, "telaesthesia."

You have these endowments: cosmaesthesia, a sense of relationship, and telaesthesia, a sense of consequences. But Robert Frost speaks the truth when he says that a full half of life cannot be reduced to a science. In art and letters, in religion and poetry there are describable skills, but the touch that makes art immortal, the spark of genius that illuminates the ages, cannot be described or defined or evaluated. So it is, too, with intuition.

As a matter of fact, more knowledge of intuition comes from a sensitive appreciation of it than from any technical study. In dissecting it, the vital pulse beat is lost. I have long loved the lines of Walt Whitman:

> When I heard the learn'd astronomer;
> When the proofs, the figures, were ranged in columns
>   before me;
> When I was shown the charts and diagrams, to add, divide,
>   and measure them;
> When I, sitting, heard the astronomer, where he lectured
>   with much applause in the lecture room,
> How soon, unaccountable, I became tired and sick;
> Till rising and gliding out, I wander'd off by myself,
> In the mystical moist night-air, and from time to time,
> Look'd up in perfect silence at the stars.

Pristine quiet and wonderment and enjoyment indeed opened the doors to a better understanding of the firmament.

Old Simeon of the New Testament waited for years in the temple, his eyes growing increasingly dim as he looked for what his heart—not logic or reason—told him God was going to send into the world. After waiting so long, a carpenter from Nazareth, with his wife and their first-born son, came to the temple. Simeon had seen similar families many times. To most, that father and mother and child looked like the others who came to the sacred place. There was a simplicity, a dignity, a devout faith about them. But had not hundreds of others been the same? Yet old Simeon moved with an unaccustomed quickness to their side and took the child lovingly in his arms. There was unwonted animation and clarity in his crackling voice: "Lord, now lettest thou thy servant depart in peace; according to thy word." Simeon knew that the answer to the longing and hoping of his people was in the child held so tenderly in his arms.

That kind of knowing—the intuitive sense that puts things in place and tells us what is important; the feeling for the essence of things—is one of the rarest and most precious gifts given to man. To be used fully, it must be developed thoughtfully, with care and sensitivity. As we learn to see relationships of problems, results of actions, the essence of life's meaning, we will gain in self-mastery.

Keeping our eyes open is a simple but important part of intuition. We must not become dull or bored or tired. Simeon would not have had the experience that lighted his soul with its glow at the very end of his life if he had said one day, "I'm too old, too tired. I no longer feel keen about going to the temple and continuing the long search." His undimmed eagerness, his watching and waiting, enabled him to perceive what the other observers could not see. The Scripture says it was "by the spirit." And so it was.

Sir William Rowan Hamilton, who made many significant discoveries and contributions in the field of mathematics said that a basic problem for him came to a solution as he "was walking with Lady Hamilton to Dublin, and came up to Brougham Bridge." Does that seem inappropriate or impossible? Well, it is not. Such a flash of insight does not necessarily depend on where you are or what you are doing. It comes unheralded, out of nowhere. But, of course, the way has been prepared. There is an inner awareness, a waiting, a receptiveness that is able to recognize the flash of truth when it comes.

An old friend has told me, across the years, of many amazing and rewarding experiences with individuals. His insights into the vast and complicated patterns within the family of man are fascinating and stimulating. Why is it so? He has cultivated a keen sensitiveness to his fellow men. In a hotel lobby or on a train he will speak to his neighbor, selecting a topic that he senses may be of interest. It may be education or world peace or transportation or the influences on the stock market. Whatever he has garnered in the way of insights about people has been due to the seeds he has sown.

An ever-increasing awareness enables us to have a moment of intuition at the most unexpected times. Every experience becomes a laboratory that may reveal a secret. I don't think we Americans fully appreciate how broad and deep were the sensibilities of Lincoln to the problems not only of the nation but of all people everywhere. We know that on a trip down the Mississippi, early in his career, he observed the practices of slavery. He looked, he felt, he evaluated, and insights and convictions were formed that later were to guide the nation.

A man, before he died a frightful alcoholic death, told me of his failure to respond to the voice of intuition. Years earlier, when he was starting to drink heavily, he had a dream that clearly predicted the tragic end to which he finally came. He felt the challenge to give up alcohol, but too long ago had he abandoned life's challenges and he was too weakened to heed the warning of his intuition.

Youth is the time to make preparations, to develop alertness, awareness, but it is never too late to learn the technique of letting your insight guide you and spur you on to better things. The man or woman who is sensitive and keeps many avenues of life open will make the most of the flash of intuition, when it comes. In turn, intuition comes most freely to those who have made themselves accessible. Little wonder that Wagner, always looking for new ideas for operas, caught the roar and excitement of a storm at sea and then wrote *The Flying Dutchman*. Mendelssohn also experienced a similar sensation while exploring a cave on the Scottish coast. Listening to the sounds and reverberations of the lapping waters, he heard and held the inspiration for his *Hebrides Overture*.

Louis Daguerre, who opened the door to the whole field of photography, did so, someone might say, because of a chance insight. It wasn't altogether true. He was convinced that there was an answer to his problem. It is quite plain that the persistence that made him try one chemical after another, hoping to sensitize a glass plate and hold an image, had a great part in it.

Madame Curie knew that uranium shed light rays but she could find no reason for it. We could, for effect, emphasize just that one luminous moment when a new element was discovered. But we would gloss over the long, hard years of painstaking work with pitchblende; we would neglect the patience and perseverance it took to accumulate one vial of radium no larger than the eraser on a pencil. The epoch-making advances made by man have demanded insight and faith and persistence of the individual, just as self-mastery demands these things of you for successful living.

A change of pace is always important to the conscious and the subconscious, which need the stimuli of varied experiences and motions and influences to quicken intuition.

The railroad employee who sits on the bench at the station as well as in his office is seeing his work from a different viewpoint, at a different pace, which—if he is observant—will make him susceptible to fresh ideas that the old routine did not provide.

I also recommend the practice of finding a time to just be quiet. It's a suggestion I make because it gives us a break in the day's fast pace, which many of us set for ourselves. Just sit quietly alone for one hour. Be perfectly still. Empty your mind of all thought. See nothing; hear nothing. Let complete peace and calm reign. When you go back to your day's occupation, you will feel refreshed, receptive.

Churchgoing is important in our lives because it provides that needed change of pace for our bodies, our minds, our spirits. As we enter that sanctuary, we are exposed to all kinds of stimuli; if we are ready, there are forces that can stir our imagination, touch our hearts, release our intuition.

Some of my most helpful sermons have come to me when my imagination was piqued or my mind was stimulated to wander off seeking some inner moment of truth. And while in recent years I have been more often in the pulpit than in the pew, I have never gone to a church service, however poor the place, and found the doors of perception closed to me.

It has been beautifully said, "Prepare the vessel and the spirit will descend." Our vessel is prepared as we move about in different environments and make it receptive to new and fresh influences.

We could probe this matter of intuition all our life and still have no scientific formula to describe it. We are nearer its dynamic source when we consider the biblical references to the Holy Spirit, that active sense of God, moving in and through us, making us patient, receptive, aware.

John Calvin wrote a comprehensive theology, known as *The Institutes,* with tremendous care. Those volumes still

serve as a basic and definitive analysis of doctrine for millions
of Protestants who are in the Presbyterian and Reformed
tradition. Calvin was a lawyer, and as you read his manu-
script you are impressed by the logic, order, and reason in
his thoughts and writings. Time after time, in a discussion of
a particular aspect of belief, to the determinative element,
he acknowledges the power of the holy spirit. That all-
powerful force—which we have labeled intuition—when it
enters a man's soul and gives him religious certainty, Calvin
sees as God's active agent.

Speaking of the Bible, he says you can respect its majesty,
you can appreciate its literary content, but "it never seriously
affects us till it is confirmed by the Spirit in our hearts."
When the persuasion comes, the mind rests with a security
that is impervious to any doubt and is stronger than any reason. A man *knows!* The Spirit has been confirmed in the
mind and, Calvin adds, it is sealed in the heart.

Let me share with you these words from *The Institutes,*
Book Three, Chapter II, Section vii:

> Now the human mind, blinded and darkened as it is, is very
> far from being able to penetrate and attain to a knowledge of
> the Divine will; and the heart also, fluctuating in perpetual
> hesitation, is far from continuing unshaken in that persuasion.
> Therefore our mind must be illuminated, and our heart estab-
> lished by some exterior power, that the word of God may obtain
> full credit with us. Now, we shall have a complete definition of
> faith, if we say, that it is a steady and certain knowledge of the
> Divine benevolence toward us, which, being founded on the
> truth of the gratuitous promise in Christ, is *both revealed to
> our minds, and confirmed to our hearts, by the Holy Spirit.*

The logician John Stuart Mill said that the "truths known
by intuition are the original premises from which all others
are inferred." Is this not so? Ask yourself what is important
and what it is that we are really talking about here and now.

What are the basic premises of your life? What do you believe?

"I believe . . ." someone says, "no, it's more than belief: I *know* that God is."

"How do you know? Prove it to me."

"I don't need to prove it. It has gripped the core of my deepest awareness. One day I was surer than I am of anything that in Jesus Christ is the redemptive power to free me from sin and guilt. From an aimless wanderer I was made a voyager on the waters of God's everlasting mercy and peace."

"Oh come now. Don't tell me that! How did it happen?"

"Beyond a certain point I cannot explain! I find that I don't need to explain it to you or myself or anybody else. This I know: It *does* happen. It *did* happen. I can say to you, as I say to myself, 'The spirit blows where it listeth.' In a moment my seeking, my struggling was at an end. I found one rock of sureness and steadiness on which to stand when all else was shifting sand—the rock of faith."

There is little to be added to this vast and beautiful and mysterious fact of human experience. Guard and treasure your gift of intuition. For here, however faltering and flickering its glow, it is the final lamp unto our feet. With this light one can explore the heights and the depths of life's ultimate meaning. Here is the light to point your way to peace of soul.

X

OVERCOMING
THE DARK OPPONENTS
WHO CHALLENGE THE WAY

. . . though I walk through the valley of the shadow . . . thy rod and thy staff they comfort me . . .

Psalms 23:4

. . . diet yourself well on . . . the biography of good and great men. See how little a space one sorrow really makes in life. See scarce a page, perhaps, given to some grief similar to your own, and how triumphantly the life sails on beyond it.

Bulwer-Lytton

He that wrestles with us strengthens our nerves and sharpens our skill. Our antagonist is our helper.

Burke

In case of any difficulty remember that God, like a gymnastic trainer, has pitted you against a rough antagonist. For what end? That you may be an Olympic conqueror, and this cannot be without toil.

Epictetus

Less pure had been the gums which the odorous balsam gives, if it had not been cut by the knife of the Arabian Sheperd.

Metastasio

Kites rise against and not with the wind . . . No man ever worked his passage anywhere in a dead calm.

John Neal

Our greatest men . . . reveal to us a life whose glory is not in the absence of suffering, but in the fact that its sufferings have been made creative, transmuted into the stuff of life itself.

Rabindranath Tagore

I THINK YOU WILL AGREE that, in religious literature, the 23rd Psalm holds a unique position in the appreciation of men. It has haunting beauty. It is rich with a fine
patina that only time can give. Revered by the centuries, it
touches the deepest sensitivity and affinities of man's soul. In
it is music, poetry, perfect prose, all fused by universal longing and experience.

But its final test lies not in its age, its beauty, its coloration,
but rather in the quality of its tone. It has relevance to man's
need. Its precious worth is not just in the sound of its words,
or in the number of times it's been read, or in the way it is
hallowed by familiarity and repetition. It speaks truth. It has
traversed the hard road of life across centuries and speaks of
the totality of man's experience. Happy and comforting moments are present, but also the knowledge that man's high
idealism and purpose lose strength and need replenishment.
Life is not all sweetness and light; there are shadows, enemies, mortal danger. The Psalm does not omit one aspect of
life.

Recently a woman visited the community I live in. After
some days she said, "I've never been in a town, to my recollection, where I've met so many widows." I don't know statis-
tically how many there are relative to other areas. There are
many. But this can be said with certainty, that each of those
women could tell of some occasion when at one moment the
path seemed to stretch out ahead, relatively untroubled.

Then, behold, the whole picture was suddenly changed. The future became clouded and uncertain. A dark opponent blocked the way.

In one way or another, sorrow, tragedy, disappointment, failure, stand unexpectedly and forbiddingly before us. Our children fail the goal they set for themselves, or they fall below the standard we had dreamed for them. Disease or age dulls our senses. The energy of youth is subdued by the burden of the years. War calls, or poverty drains, or weakness betrays, and suddenly a silent, strong force challenges our way.

We can't talk about any mastery of life without considering such times of hardship. We must be prepared for difficulty. To be successful we must make weapons and school ourselves in methods of defense. But how? What are the steps and secrets here?

First of all, we can accept the fact that, in one form or another, as the 23rd Psalm suggests, some distressing deal is in the cards for us all. Forearmed with this knowledge, we must believe that we are capable of meeting and facing obstacles, and we must strengthen our inner fortifications.

On this matter of preparation, look at two of the heroes of history. Here are two men who dealt masterfully with life, first of all because they had prepared themselves. One is known as David, a shepherd boy. He is seen in his early years guarding his sheep, learning to use his sling to protect his flock. But more than that, he is absorbing the quiet and solemnity of nature. He is learning the wisdom of the natural world and the wisdom of man. He is growing in the fear of the Lord.

Now turn to another scene in his life, one in dramatic contrast to the quiet picture of the boy tending his lambs. Now he stands before the giant Goliath, who has terrified the legions of King Saul. The little shepherd lad goes out alone to meet the enemy. Behold, there is an astonishing and unexpected victory. A miracle is wrought. The giant falls before David's sling. Then that shepherd boy, so insignificant in the back meadows with the flock, goes on to become Israel's most illustrious king. His courage and faith and steadiness and vision help to expand and stabilize a whole people. But do not forget his days of preparation, when, as a shepherd, he was quietly growing in strength.

Turn to a page from the history of our own country. When the very foundations of our corporate life were shaken during the Civil War, the man who led the nation through to peace was one who had long been schooled in the hardships of frontier life. From the rigors of log-cabin and rail-splitting days, from disappointment in romance, from difficulties met in the daily struggle with poverty, from defeat at elections, from the discipline of himself and other men, he learned that life was tears as well as laughter.

The competent individual in any field is known by his ability to meet emergencies. The experienced surgeon performs an exacting operation. All seems to be going well. But at a particularly crucial moment the patient's pulse begins to fail and his life is in jeopardy. But the long, silent study of years, together with more years of building up experience, have made that doctor fitted for moments like this. Quick orders are given. Decisive action follows firm decision. The patient's strength is restored and he lives.

Look into the courtroom. The question between the contenders is important. The masterful lawyer has carefully prepared his case. His brief is ready, the procedure is visualized in his mind, and the groundwork for the steps in his presentation has been laid with thoroughness. But the unexpected happens. The testimony of a witness suddenly puts a different slant on the facts. A bit of evidence is introduced that was not anticipated. The case, with its important consequences can be lost. But that trial expert was made for issues like this. Out of his silent times of thought and preparation have come versatility and judgment to cope with any eventuality. He changes his emphasis in presentation. The seemingly important factors are met head-on and reduced to inconsequential size before the larger issues they at first seemed to weaken. The case, and the cause it represents, is won because there was preparation to meet any difficulty that might challenge him.

It is wise to admit to yourself that in one form or another the dark opponent will, at some time, block the way. And your preparation gains a step forward when you accept the fact that all of us were made to endure and survive trouble. This is amazingly verified by what we are physiologically. Our physical organs are built to meet unexpected trials. One lung can be lost. The heart may be impaired. The liver may not function fully. The major portion of the pancreas, we are told, can be removed, and still sufficient alkaline secretion is produced to carry on the basic process of digestion. Yet the physical organism can still live. It is equally true that, as we are physiologically able to continue, so are we able to do mentally and spiritually. There is much truth in the adage, "No burden is put upon us that we do not have the strength to bear."

We were made not merely to uneventfully plod along the road of life; we were made to do battle with unexpected assailants of sorrow and opposition and find comfort and hope and renewed strength in overcoming them. G. K. Chesterton once said, "For one man who wants to be comforted, a hundred want to be stirred. Men, . . . want in the last resort, not life, but drums." He's right, isn't he? To know that struggle will come, to prepare for it, and to know that this is what we were made for, is an indispensable basis for any victory in life.

The importance of these matters cannot be overemphasized when we think of the development of our own character and our children's. We certainly are reaping an unhappy harvest in the generation that has had a weak and libertine education, with its minimal emphasis on discipline and the need to be strong and prepared. In 1941 Will Durant wrote with feeling and fire, "The result is an adolescent without responsibility, a maturity without character; and . . . our children will not thank us for the liberty of their youth. To exact nothing of a child that its intellect cannot understand and approve is the depth of nonsense to which some of us dedicated ourselves in the days of our dreams. Parents must learn again to command, to assign duties and see to it that they are performed; they must not be ashamed to require— and must fit themselves to deserve filial respect . . ." It is the externally imposed and inwardly accepted discipline that has brought substantial progress in any people of history. We see it vividly, in our time, in the rapid progress and development of Soviet Russia. We must never avoid, either in personal or corporate life, coming to terms with the requirements and responsibilities that make us strong—unless we prefer to breed a generation of totally mollycoddled, confused, and aimless individuals.

No matter where we look we see the advantages of preparedness. Lord Nelson's astonishing successes came on the sea because of his insistence on being forearmed. What hardship and hard work he demanded of himself and his men! But the confidence and skill in battle were rooted in the discipline that he had imposed on himself and his men. It mattered not that his opponents were idle in their port; he and his navy were tirelessly training at sea. On the occasion when he learned that Villeneuve had returned to Toulon because of bad weather be exclaimed, "These gentlemen are not accustomed to the Gulf of Lyons gales, but we have buffeted them for twenty-one months without carrying away a spar."

Struggle and opposition are our lot in life—and the only

way to meet them masterfully is to know that they will come
and diligently prepare for them.

But let us keep in mind that we were made only for
conflict; it is in how we meet opposition that determines the
real measure of our mastery.

When we read a biography of a famous man, one of our
first questions is: How did he start? Tell us about it. That is
always an interesting part of a book. But more interesting
still is how he ended up. We are willing to read about the
fair breezes that blew him along his course. But tell us of the
storms! That's the drama and excitement that bring us to
the edge of our seats. That part moves us most because it tells
us of the stuff of which he was made.

We are touched, as Jesus speaks the words of the Sermon
on the Mount. We can see clearly in our mind's eye the place
where He purportedly spoke those immortal truths. To the
north can be seen the snow-covered peak of Mount Hermon.
Southward the River Jordon begins its major flow to the
Dead Sea. The slope where the Master stands inclines gently
to touch the waters of Lake Galilee. Hundreds listen, with
loving attention; there is a lifting up of hearts. Jesus and His
listeners are wrapped in glory and exhilaration that cannot
be fully explained by any of them. We listen with those who
are there. We breathe the air they do, and it has a new fresh-
ness and stimulation. We walk away with them, His spirit
giving a new dimension to our life. We, with all who are
there, know that this man is, indeed, a Master.

But in the narrow, twisting streets of Jerusalem, where
people spat upon Him, where His shoulders sag under the
burden of a cross, where blood trickles into His eyes to
mingle with the salt of His tears of pain, we are moved to a
feeling that Galilee could not evoke. Look at Him! In silence,
in spite of the mockery and cruelty, He keeps going. We fall
on our knees in His most terrible but most majestic hour.

He gave us immortality in this life, but we do not purchase it with our comfort but with our pain.

All who know the past history of Mormonism, together with the discipline and dedication that mark that religious order, have great respect for it. Something of the original vitality of Brigham Young still flows through it. Recall that man's early life. It was marked by suffering under extreme poverty and living by the standards of a strict moral code. Brigham spent only twelve days in school and Vardis Fisher has written, "During the remainder of his boyhood he chopped cordwood, plowed and planted and reaped, going barefoot most of the time and in rags, but keeping his will unbroken and his mind serene. His father often punished him, giving him a blow first and a warning afterward, because his son often walked on Sunday, not for exercise but for pleasure." Out of that stern background came the strong resources to lead those "children of God," across the plains, facing devastating hardship and opposition, to Utah. Because Brigham Young had met and mastered obstacles, because he had mastered himself, he created some of the finest dignity and glories of the Mormon faith.

The man who has really mastered himself will look at difficulties and opposition not with fear but with exhilaration and anticipation. The New Testament speaks of "glorying in tribulation" because "tribulation worketh patience; and patience, experience; and experience, hope: and hope maketh not ashamed."

We have to live with ourselves. To live with a self that has been fearful of trouble, that has evaded hardships, that has weakly compromised instead of honestly struggling against evil, can produce no happiness or pleasure. Our conscience gives us a glow of inner dignity when we can say to ourselves that we have, when life demanded it, pulled with vigor and determination against the tide.

The truth is that our physical and mental and spiritual nerves are most keyed up, are sharpest, when we face difficulty. I have a friend who is a flier. He has told me of hazardous flights during the war and of storms and sleet in more recent times. I've always been impressed how alive his eyes become, how animated his voice, as he describes those moments. Once he was asked why he found such satisfaction in those experiences. His response was, "Why, I suppose that then I had the feeling most of all that I was alive."

We have been made to survive just about any foe except success. When there is no feeling of opposition, when the imagination visualizes no contender who will rise up to offer his fearsome challenge, then life softens up. Phillips Brooks expressed it this way: "Bad will be the day for every man when he becomes absolutely contented with the life that he is living, with the thoughts that he is thinking, with the deeds that he is doing, when there is not forever beating at the doors of his soul some great desire to do something larger."

It is the answer to a challenge keeps us from falling into the slough of idle content. With a purpose that is beyond ourselves, with the keying up of our energies and resources, we find that life has a vitality and meaning.

To believe that we are born into this world for some good and constructive purpose, and to move forward, enables us to take what opposition or failure there may be without succumbing to it. We may fail or seem to be subdued, but only momentarily. The cause for which we are struggling is greater than ourselves, and the struggle itself, be it successful or unavailing, is inconsequential.

You see this masterful strength in a man like Lincoln. Harsh criticism and stinging opposition surrounded and confronted him. Yet he moved with dignity and strength and steadiness. The outward barbs did not wound him inwardly.

His purpose in life was his shield. One may wonder how so many individuals, facing vast tides of opposition, can still move forward with such resolution and will. The only answer seems to be the fact that they are committed to a cause that transcends their own brief lives.

Something of heroic quality is felt in the apostle Paul. He was a prisoner; his end was near. His cell, bare and inhospitable, was in total contrast to the glory of the Roman Empire around him. A citizen of Rome, he could have made compromises and adjusted to the pleasures and outward trappings of Roman civilization. But something stronger claimed him. A purpose gripped and dominated him that would not let him go. By giving his life for what he believed in, now stands out more masterfully across the centuries than the rich and the idle and the briefly successful of gilded Rome. His words touch the depths of every sensitive and sincere soul, "I have fought a good fight—I have kept the faith."

I have stood under the awesome shadow of the Parthenon in Athens and looked at the great stone drums that Alexander the Great, before he began his victorious campaigns, pointed out to his generals. There was a great purpose that kindled his imagination. So successfully did he transmit his vitality and intensity to his associates that the difficulties and obstacles and opposition that lay before him were as nothing before the bravery and daring to meet and overcome it till the world was conquered. Alexander the Great was magnificent as he stood on the Acropolis at Athens. But at the end of his career, with purpose and meaning disintegrated, he died a dissolute death. He failed because he had lacked what sustained Paul to the bitter end; a cause beyond himself that would enable him to say finally, "I have fought a good fight—I have kept the faith."

We meet life masterfully when there is knowledge and a growing conviction that God is and that He is with us. This is the ultimate source of power to meet the dark opponents on the way.

Let me share with you a few sentences from an unexpected letter that I received from a man in Lancashire, England. Having read my book, *Personal Security Through Faith,* he expressed sincere appreciation, and then went on to say, ". . . perhaps most of us, like myself, are turned to the search for a really secure way of life because of some trouble.

"And it is, perhaps, after trouble that security seems so far away. When we have health and ability to work, we believe that we can earn our own security without any help—either from above or below. When we lose our health we tend at first to think that we are at the end and without hope.

"Perhaps, . . . serious illnesses which curtail our activities for more than a short period—are sent to us merely that we shall start to search for the real truth of being. *All I know is that I have been forced—almost, perhaps, against my will—to take the first steps in throwing my whole being on the mercy and strength of God.* [Italics mine.] He is caring for me always. I know that now, though two or three years ago I would probably have laughed at the idea. Indeed, He is caring for me so well that at the age when most men moan that they are beginning to be unemployable, I am giving up my business and starting a new career."

To have the sense of God's spirit and purpose in our lives does for any man what it has done for our friend from England. New frontiers are opened. Other people are inspired. Those who follow in the way that has been blazed are enabled to go further than would have been the case otherwise.

There's evidence to show that our Pilgrim Fathers thought that the land inward from the coast was without any value. To them it was an impassable forest. Up to the time of George Washington the Alleghenies were regarded as a barrier over which men would not, and felt they could not, pass. As a matter of fact, Patrick Henry likened the Allegheny

Mountains to the Alps that separated European nations, and he said that "mountain ranges are lines that God has set to separate one people from another."

One of the most thrilling chapters in our history is the record of those who opened the way, who found the passes, who built the tunnels and bridges and roads and the machines that enabled men to move over the seemingly impossible barriers. The stark and lonely places of the world, which seemed to be impossible to penetrate, have been conquered through man's efforts.

As our lives have been enriched by the inspiration of others who have gone before, so we are compelled, by God's spirit, to do the same for those who follow. In doing so, we are strengthened by the realization that, in meeting our hardships with patience and courage and confidence, we achieve some of our deepest insights and the richest fulfillment. We can look back over the hard and bitter days and years of struggle and count them among our best.

The other day I received a letter from a woman in the Midwest who wrote of her hard and sorrowful times. Then she added, "What understanding and sensitiveness I have acquired through the years came most of all from those milestones that mark my darkest times." There is wisdom in her words. Those who go through their dark hours with hope and calmness will find that they are milestones marking their surest moments of progress.

There are three ways that prepare us for life's trials. One is the Spartan way that says, "I have strength within me to do it. 'I am the captain of my soul.' With the courage and will that is mine, I will master be when the struggle comes."

Another way is in the spirit of Socrates, who affirmed that we have minds, reason, and judgment to evaluate and help us cope with the enigmas and struggles of life.

The Christian way is the third approach. It doesn't exclude the first two, but it adds, "You don't begin with yourself, your will, or your reason. You begin with God, who is the beginning and the end. When your strength grows weak and your reason fails you, faith in the Creator gives you the power to overcome all things."

We need the presence of God's spirit in the midst of our struggles. That inner quiet gives us a relief from uncertainty, from tension, from fear. Gone is our concern about what others may think; we stand true to ourselves and what is of ultimate value.

Jesus of Nazareth, standing before the tribunal, about to be crucified, was a victim of man's ignorance and brutality. Yet He was quiet; there was an absence of bitterness or complaint. His inner mastery, that had developed through the years, reached its superb climax in the agony of the Garden of Gethsemane. Through tortured hours He came to the invincible conviction, "Not my will, but thine be done."

We need to be honest with ourselves and admit that, in the last analysis, our ultimate source of power comes not from within ourselves, but from God. Alexander Miller, in *The Renewal of Man,* put it this way: "The human dilemma calls not for a resolve but for a rescue." The man who stands with mastery before life's dilemmas is the man of intellectual strength and conviction, securely girded with will and reason. But as the years go by, he will fail, his wounds and scars will increase—the battle is unending. His will grows weak; his energy wanes; his doubts grow more pressing when his sense of purpose and direction has grown dim and he is ever more aware of his weaknesses and his defeats; he can no longer respond as he once did. The only answer for him is in the awareness that "Underneath are the everlasting arms." He sees that he has had a small part in building the universe; he has moved forward a little bit and made the way somewhat easier for others who follow. And his self-mastery, his final peace, rest on the belief in God, who sees the over-all purpose in creation.

XI

THE ENNOBLING
POWER
OF PATIENCE

. . . let patience have her perfect work. . . . be swift to hear, slow to speak, slow to wrath.

James 1:4, 19

By their patience and perseverance God's children are truly known from hypocrites and dissemblers.

Augustine

Never think that God's delays are God's denials. Hold on! hold fast! hold out! Patience is genius.

Count de Buffon

Adopt the pace of nature: her secret is patience.

Emerson

Patience and gentleness are power.

Leigh Hunt

Patience; accomplish thy labor; accomplish thy work of affection! Sorrow and silence are strong, and patient endurance is godlike. Therefore accomplish thy labor of love, till the heart is made godlike,
Purified, strengthened, perfected and rendered more worthy of heaven.

Longfellow

They also serve who only stand and wait.

Milton

He that has patience may compass anything.

François Rabelais

Endurance is nobler than strength, and patience than beauty.

Ruskin

He that will have a cake of the wheat must needs tarry the grinding.

Shakespeare

Our grandparents did more repeating of old axioms, more reading of wise sayings, than do we moderns. Copybooks of students from the nineteenth century contain adages and poems written by youngsters, who thereby gained spiritual inspiration as well as improved skill in penmanship. In our home is a book, profusely illustrated and beautifully set in clear type, that was published in the nineties. It bears the title, *The Ideal Life—the Royal Road to Success and Happiness*. On the cover, bordered with lilies, is a picture of a Victorian family seated before a fireplace. Its six hundred pages are devoted to the qualities that make for the good life. Among its finest sections is a full treatment of one of the cardinal virtues that is indispensable to life's mastery. A few light verses by Mary F. Van Dyck identify it. They read:

> There is a little plant that grows
> In almost every soil,
> If he who sows the seed bestows
> A little care and toil
>
> Though needful as the constant food
> That daily want supplies,
> Like every other common good,
> We fail the plant to prize.
>
> Till absence of it proves its worth,
> And discord holds its sway;
> And crosses incident to earth,
> Grow heavier every day.

Well call it "Patience," kind to three
That would redeem the fall,
Blest Faith, and Hope, and Charity,
We surely need them all!

I've been told by a native of the eastern part of America
that in many a kitchen of the sturdy New England house-
holds there grew a "patience" plant, cultivated where busy
hands toiled all day. When evening came and spirits may
have been at low ebb, the plant spoke its simple and ele-
mental lesson: patience. That little plant may very well have
played its part in developing the fine-grained New England
character.

A boy, who was informed that oaks grow out of acorns,
planted an acorn in the earth, and the next day, eager to see
what was happening, he dug it up again. He repeated the
process for a whole week, but still no oak appeared. "It isn't
true," he cried, "it doesn't happen. No oak tree come from
the acorn."

"My son," said an older and wiser man, "it will happen.
But it takes time. Rain and sun and warmth and quietness
and many days and weeks must pass before the acorn unlocks
its secret heart to begin the oak. You have to be patient to
see it. And 'twill take all the years of your life till it stands
a great tree against the sky."

In your travels you may have stood before the bronze doors
of the impressive Romanesque baptistry in Florence. There
you will have admired the work of Ghiberti. Each panel of
those majestic doors is a masterpiece. You may be moved to
say, "What vision, what genius, created these!"

True—but only in part, my friend. It took twenty years of
patient labor till the vision was translated into that ageless
bronze.

Patience is not acquiescence. It is not a quiet subservience
and indifference. It is active orientation and growth of mind

and strengthening of emotions. It requires that we know
where we are going and that we know the difficulties on the
way. Patience, which negates wasting time in quick and irra-
tional spurts of energy or wandering aimlessly along byways
instead of pursuing the intended goal, is indispensable to
fulfillment.

All of us have seen the disaster that results from lack
of patience. People are hurt because someone could not restrain a sharp word, a hurried judgment. A business can fail
because someone, impatient for results, insists on overex-
pansion.

We live in times when Howard Thurman's lines from
"Deep Is the Hunger" speak for many:

Always I have an underlying anxiety about things.
Sometimes I am in a hurry to achieve my ends
And am completely without patience. It is hard for me to
    realize that some growth is slow.
That all processes are not swift. I cannot always discriminate
Between what takes time to develop and what can be rushed,
. . .　　　　　. . .　　　　　. . .
O to understand the meaning of perspective . . .

But it is not too late to acquire patience and benefit from
its application in our daily lives.

A quiet, restrained approach to any situation, to any task,
to any problem, is the essence of patience.

Pavlov, one of Russia's greatest scientists, just before his
death at the age of eighty-seven, wrote a bequest to the aca-
demic youth of his nation. Although his prime interests lay
in science, his counsel is by no means restricted to that field.
He wrote:

What can I wish to the youth of my country who devote
themselves to science?

Firstly, gradualness. About this most important condition of
fruitful scientific work I never can speak without emotion. . . .

From the very beginning of your work, school yourselves to severe gradualness in the accumulation of knowledge.

Learn the ABC of science before you try to ascend to its summit. Never begin the subsequent without mastering the preceding. Never attempt to screen an insufficiency of knowledge even by the most audacious surmise and hypothesis. Howsoever this soap-bubble will rejoice your eyes by its play, it inevitably will burst and you will have nothing except shame.

School yourselves to demureness and patience. Learn to inure yourselves to drudgery in science. Learn, compare, collect the facts!

Perfect as is the wing of a bird, it never could raise the bird up without resting on air. Facts are the air of a scientist. Without them you never can fly. Without them your "theories" are vain efforts.

But learning, experimenting, observing, try not to stay on the surface of the facts. Do not become the archivists of facts. Try to penetrate to the secret of their occurrence, persistently search for the laws which govern them.

Clearly, there is a wisdom in those words that each of us can seek to use, regardless of our profession or way of life.

We are able to endure many irritations that are not worth bothering about, if we would but try. The patience of Jesus should be the supreme example that we keep before us as we go through each day, saying to ourselves, "I will keep feeding my mind and heart with such a spirit."

Some time ago, on a rainy day, as I drove through a long stretch of quiet countryside, I turned on the car radio. Fibber McGee was outlining to Molly an exciting and ambitious plan to produce a spectacular motion picture that would out-DeMille DeMille. It was to be staged in the garage which would be the studio. There were to be ten people in the cast. The back yard was to be the set. There were to be conflicts between vast ancient armies. In answer to Molly's insistent and sensible questioning, Fibber said that by trick photography, repeating and splicing the film many times, the illusion of vastness and numbers would be created. Molly finally pointed out that, even if all this was possible, he would still run into trouble because each member would want to be the star. Fibber pondered that a moment, obviously deflated, then replied, "Molly, that's the trouble with the world today. Nobody's willing to be a spear carrier any more."

It may be exhilarating to play a starring role in life, but there is steady satisfaction in doing the quiet, unheralded work, patiently, lovingly. We should make use of the power of humility, the spirit that is quick to hear and feel, but slow to speak, slow to anger.

A situation can easily disintegrate into chaos if we try to force things. Impatience brings in its wake many negative and destructive aftereffects. Dr. Leland D. Hinsie, in a discussion of the methods of training children, points out that parents should be in no great hurry. Successful management of children comes by calm reasoning, by repetition, and by a schooling that extends over a period of several years. He says, "What parents do not commonly understand is that forming a character is . . . a slow process and that character can be remarkably distorted by neglect or oversolicitude or by forcing." He then added, "We overlook the fact that it takes time to make a mother and a father."

If we consider some of our own personal experiences, we will have to admit that in many situations we have reacted badly to pressure from someone else. Therefore we should try to keep that fact in mind when we find ourselves impatiently pressuring others.

How often I have counseled individuals whose marriages have been badly shaken. I shall never forget the poignant regret of one man who said, "I wish to God that I had been able to control my impatience. It wasn't that I didn't have a good wife. I did. But my self-centered picture of what I thought she ought to be made me force issues that hurt her so deeply and so continuously that the damage is now beyond repair." He learned, too late, one of the fundamental rules for self-mastery.

One of the greatest Biblical passages is from the Gospel of Luke, "In your patience ye shall win your souls." It is good for a man to know that he may win his own security, his own integrity, the flowering of his own selfhood, not by strife, but by patience.

The surest foundation for patience is having the perspective of eternity. We must be certain of the end before we can travel the distance, through light and dark, through good times and bad, with confidence and serenity. When we grow weary, we are apt to forget that there is an over-all meaning of life, a meaning we can never fully grasp. At these times do we most need patience and an abiding faith in God. "A thousand years in His sight," says the Psalmist, "are but as yesterday when it is past . . ."

The Church was not built in our time, nor in a few hundred years of history. It goes back to the dawn of conscience, to that moment when man, standing upright, knew that he had a mind and a soul. It enshrines the heroism, inspiration, insight that lighted the centuries. And it must be preserved for future generations, who will seek to live by that light. Something of the perspective of God is here, quietly, insistently calling men in every era to strive for the truth till there exists on earth a true brotherhood of man. How patiently God must watch us and work through us!

There is a patience that has created miracles of order about us, that has wrought wonders of harmony in the cosmos and awesome structures of faith and hope in the seeking mind and soul of man. Wherever we look we are reminded that we are a part of a creation where patience is indispensable to any perfect work. In our quest for knowledge of ourselves, of the world, in our efforts to bring justice and righteousness and truth to all men, we must also seek patience. We will find that in the spirit of God that is in our soul.

XII

MASTERY
AS A CITIZEN
IN THE SOVEREIGN
KINGDOM OF GOD

. . . and there were great voices in heaven, saying, The Kingdoms of this world are become the Kingdoms of our Lord . . . and he shall reign forever and ever.

Revelation 11:15

As a man is, so is his God; therefore God was so often an object of mockery.

Goethe

God governs the world, and we have only to do our duty wisely, and leave the issue to Him.

John Jay

The God of metaphysics is but an idea. But the God of religion, the maker of heaven and earth, the sovereign Judge of actions and thoughts, is a power.

Joubert

To God belongeth the east and the west; therefore, whithersoever ye turn yourselves to pray, there is the word of God; for God is omnipresent and omniscient.

Koran

History is the revelation of of Providence.

Kossuth

If thou hast wanderings in the wilderness and find'st no Sinai, 'tis thy soul is poor.

Lowell

A voice is in the wind I do not know;
A meaning on the face of the high hills
Whose utterance I cannot comprehend,
A something is behind them: that is God.

George MacDonald

All laws suppose a lawgiver, and . . . all working involves a Divine energy.

Alexander Maclaren

S HORTLY BEFORE HIS DEATH in 1911, Sam Walter
Foss composed these lines under the title, "Two Gods":

A boy was born 'mid little things,
  Between a little world and sky—
And dreamed not of the cosmic rings
  Round which the circling planets fly.

He lived in little works and thoughts,
  Where little ventures grow and plod,
And paced and ploughed his little plots,
  And prayed unto his little God.

But as the mighty system grew,
  His faith grew faint with many scars;
The cosmos widened in his view—
  But God was lost among his stars.

II

Another boy in lowly days,
  As he, to little things was born,
But gathered lore in woodland ways,
  And from the glory of the morn.

As wider skies broke on his view,
  God greatened in his growing mind;
Each year he dreamed his God anew,
  And left his older God behind.

He saw the boundless scheme dilate,
In star and blossom, sky and clod;
And as the universe grew great,
He dreamed for it a greater God.

Those lines contain a twofold idea that no honest seeker
of truth should side-step, that no counselor who tries to help
us in our search should evade. The first idea is that man, to
a certain extent, creates his God. The other idea is that the
concept of God that a man has, helps to mold him. The
image that man creates in turn creates him.

I daresay that if you put down on paper your concept of
God, you would use some imagery of the Bible to portray
Him in terms of personality. Many of us have a picture—vague
perhaps, but nonetheless sure—of a benign, fatherly figure.

Kirsopp Lake writes: "After all, Faith is not belief in spite
of evidence, but life in scorn of consequence—a courageous
thrust in the great purpose of all things and pressing forward
to finish the work which is in sight, whatever the price may
be." Then, expressing his opinion on the concept of God in
terms of personality, he writes, "Who knows whether the
'personality' of which men talk so much and know so little
may not prove to be the temporary limitation rather than
the necessary expression of Life?" Indeed, across the centuries, scores and scores of men and women from the lowliest
to the highest intellectual circles have visualized their God
in terms of personality.

And some have described God as pure spirit, a force, a
power at work in the universe, similar to the classic definition
in the Westminster Catechism: "God is a spirit, infinite,
eternal and unchangeable . . ." Such a description is found
in Lololomai's Prayer, taken from *The Indian Book,* edited
by Natalie Curtis. The passage reads:

To whom do the Hopis pray?
It is that which makes the rain—that makes all things. It is
Power, and it lives behind the sun.

Does the Power that lives behind the sun look like a man, or like anything that the Hopis have ever seen?

No, it is not like a man; we don't know how it looks. We only know that it is.

When Lololomai, the chief, prays, how does he pray?

He goes to the edge of the cliff and turns his face to the rising sun, and scatters the sacred corn meal. Then he prays for all the people. He asks that we may have rain and corn, and that our fields may bring us plenty. He prays that all the people may have health and long life and be happy and good in their hearts. And Hopis are not the only people he prays for. He prays for everybody in the whole world—everybody. And not people alone; Lololomai prays for all the animals. And not for animals alone; he prays for the plants. He prays for everything that has life. That is how Lololomai prays.

But there are others who say, "I must be honest: I still go to church, I bow my head in prayer, and try to worship. But I have a deep personal perplexity; I ponder the chaos and evil and the irrationalism in this world and I can't help but express the taunting whisper in my mind, 'I wonder why I am here at all.' Sincerely I question whether there is a God at all. How can there be a good God, who would permit such misery and sorrow in life?"

No matter what our concept of God is—or is not—to a large degree we make it ourselves. Our idea of God is a result of our experiences, our thinking; it is constructed on the judgments, the observations, the evaluations, the conditioning, from within, and from external influences by our fellow men.

Here is a woman who says her life is shattered, her faith gone. Having lost a loved one, she now lies whimpering and helpless. You say to her, "My dear, what kind of faith did you have that it has now abandoned you? Tell me about your idea of God. What kind of God did you believe in?"

And she describes a cosmic Santa Claus whose prime intent seemed to be to look after her welfare, her comfort. Suddenly the image was smashed. The God she dreamed was inadequate.

Over there is a very religious man. There is but one religion. And he has it. He tells you that he has been washed in the blood, that he is saved. But listen to him speak further. He is bitter toward those whose religion is different from his. He is constantly plaguing his associates. He damns as pagans other Christians whose practices differ from his. Why this strange paradox? "My friend, what do you think about God?"

He outlines for you his concept of a jealous and inflexible monarch, easily angered, whose subjects must obey or they are cast into the eternal fire of hell.

We reflect in our lives the kind of God we believe in; if the concept of God is limited, that limitation is within us. Wrote Edna St. Vincent Millay:

> He whose soul is flat,
> The sky will close in on him by and by.

On the other hand, the greater your image of God, the more you will recognize and appreciate the wonder and the majesty of all creation. His compassion and forgiveness reaches into the darkest depths; his love extends to the farthest boundaries of space. The Book of Revelation describes the Divine thus: ". . . and there were great voices in heaven, saying, The Kingdoms of this world are become the Kingdoms of our Lord, . . . and he shall reign forever and ever."

It is because we create false gods and because our ideas of the Lord God Almighty are so inadequate that we have great need of the Church. It is there to teach us, to remind and guide us, to lift up to us the vision of God's sovereignty and majesty. It presents us with a truer, grander, concept of the Lord, preserving the vital religious tradition of mankind.

With that exalted and ennobling concept in our souls, we are enabled to deal more nobly and masterfully with life.

It is clear that our concept of God should be ever-growing. It requires meditation and prayer, evaluation and interpretation. For some, this is accomplished with ease. Chesterton said of St. Francis, "He ran away to God as other boys have run away to sea." However, St. Francis was an exception. For most of us, the development of a stable concept of God is a hard and painstaking business. The more common experience of man is described best by a quotation from *The Towers of Trebizond:* "We may not be taken up and transported to our journey's end, but must travel thither on foot, traversing the whole distance of the narrow way." In this task the individual and corporate experience of the Church is tremendously helpful. It keeps before us the wider ideal; it teaches us the language of symbols, which we need to understand in order to best appreciate the concept of God. Hocking, in his study, *The Meaning of God,* speaks of the idea of God as containing an "uncounted infinity," which rests upon personal experience, insight, and revelation. Through sermon and prayer, by music and poetry, the Church places that infinity before the seeking heart and mind. Each participant in the Church contributes to and takes something from it.

I'm sure you remember William Herbert Carruth's verses, "Each in His Own Tongue." Simply and tellingly he shows the different interpretations and concepts open to man's mind.

> A fire-mist and a planet—
>   A crystal and a cell,
> A jelly-fish and a Saurian,
>   And caves where the cave men dwell;
> Then a sense of law and beauty
>   And a face turned from the clod,—

Some call it Evolution,
And others call it God.

A haze on the far horizon,
The infinite, tender sky,
The ripe, rich tint of the cornfields,
And the wild geese sailing high;
And all over upland and lowland
The charm of the golden rod,—
Some of us call it Autumn,
And others call it God.

* * * *

A picket frozen on duty,
A mother starved for her brood,
Socrates drinking the hemlock,
And Jesus on the rood;
And millions who, humble and nameless,
The straight, hard pathway plod,—
Some call it Consecration
And others call it God.

It is difficult for some of us to think of "Church" as an entity when there are so many varied denominations, but basically, every Church is the House of God. The motto of the Chapel at Watch Hill, Rhode Island proclaims on its walls:

> *The Church is Many as the Waves, but One as the Sea.*
> In Essentials, Unity; in Non-Essentials, Liberty;
> in All Things, Charity.

The Church exists, with its treasury of spiritual experience, with centuries of thinking and feeling about and behind and through it, so that it can say to us, "In the deepest perceiving and knowing, it is all God. This evolving universe, the loveliness of nature, the nobility of man, all bespeak His creativeness and purpose. Sing then His glory! Bow in wonder and love and praise! Then rise to walk the ways of man, but with the majesty of eternity about you."

Are we deluding ourselves? Is the agnostic, who says, "I don't know," really more intelligent and realistic than those who affirm as fact a supposition that can't be proven? Is it all just imaginative and lovely poetry—or an opiate—and no more?

The answer is, "No." There are two things to be said. One, if there is any weight of evidence, it points to God rather than the absence of God. Secondly, accepting the idea of God, experiencing the presence of God, acting as if God did not exist.

Dr. Fosdick pointed out that it took only one footprint on Robinson Crusoe's island to lead to the undeniable conclusion that another human being was about. "You could not explain that footprint as the accidental impact of the waves upon the sand. *Someone had been there.*"

As for the evidence of God, view this vast universe and consider the sweep of history. Grant all of its evil and chaos. The amazing thing is that, amid the debris, there are some footprints on the sands of time. If there is but *one* footprint of purpose, you know that there is a Creator, who indicates a bold and a majestic purpose that can't be explained by anything else we know.

Look at the cross of Calvary. If ever there was evidence of human depravity, blindness, cowardice, ignorance, cruelty, it was there. And yet that is not how history interprets it. Behold in the courage, the compassion, the nobility in Jesus, there is an imprint that transcends evil and chaos.

You and I know about chromosomes and their chance arrangement. We are told, and accept as true, that they determine the seeming ability, character, temperament of man. That I will accept as a reasonably well-documented hypothesis. But to ask me to believe that the mind of an Einstein, or the humanitarianism of a Schweitzer, or the wisdom of a

Lincoln, or the compassion and love of Jesus, is just a fortuitous arrangement of chromosomes is to ask me to stretch my credulity too far. I cannot accept it. This is not blind accident; this reveals the spirit of God at work through man.

There are the footprints of order and law and compensation, and beauty and selflessness in man's history. It is a blind man who will say they mean nothing. It is not all just matter and motion. There is some noble purpose here! A Master has created man and his destiny.

Shakespeare says:

> There's a divinity that shapes our ends,
> Rough-hew them how we will.

James Russell Lowell exclaims:

> Truth forever on the scaffold,
>   Wrong forever on the throne,
> Yet that scaffold sways the future.

The evidence of a Divine imprint in this cosmos is in the soul of man!

To affirm this is not to accept an opiate. It does not restrain and restrict life; rather, it frees it. The unbeliever loses that broadening experience altogether. He denies himself the joy and fulfillment of a great friendship with God, which is enriched by trust. But more than that, he is forced into the limitations of not trusting. Unable to believe in anyone or anything, he will find no reason to do much of anything. He can make no choice, because he doesn't know what to choose or why. As a result he denies himself the sense of responsibility that comes from commitment. The "adventurous joy of believing" is an experience that he does not know. His skepticism and indecision can be a decisive factor in creating an opiate to his spirit.

There is a poignant tragedy for the mind and the soul of such a person. This is illustrated in the confessions of Kath-

erine Mansfield. She wrote to one correspondent, after expressing first her rejection of the idea of a personal God, and
then her longing for such a belief, "It seems to me there is
a great change come over the world since people like us believed in God. God is now gone for all of us. Yet we must
believe; and not only that—we must carry our weakness and
our sin and our devilishness to somebody. I don't mean in
a bad abasing way. But we must feel that we are known, that
our hearts are known, as God knew us. Therefore love today
between lovers has to be not only human but divine. Their
love is their religion. . . . But oh, it is no good."

Without God, a man is a mere bit of flotsam, floating, like
other scum, on an aimless, cold and indifferent sea. To the
man who believes, life has meaning and in the struggle to
go forward there is glory. There can be no sense of shattered-
ness, the sense of the fragmentariness in your life if there is
God. Rather, there is relatedness, meaning, wholeness. As
D. Elton Trueblood put it, "The only sure way in which we
can transcend our human relativities is by obedience to the
absolute and eternal God."

I know at my deepest depths that God is because I have
seen that flash of the eternal in the temporal. God did not
stoop to earth just once, to reveal Himself at Bethlehem. I
have seen Him in lives that are strengthened, lived more
usefully, more compassionately—lives that have radiance, because they have looked on Him for but an instant and seen
all of God they need to know. His love and grace has drawn
and won their love and allegiance.

One of the finest descriptions of a Christian I've come
across was composed by Charles Clayton Morrison. "A Christian could be accurately defined as one who seeks to identify
his conduct with the will of God as this will reveals itself
ever anew in living companionship with Jesus Christ." Love
and faith are the conductors through which God is communicated to the soul. The Christian sees in Jesus not acci-

dent but revelation, and the glow from eternity he sees in
his Lord enters his own heart.

Here is a quick summary of two biographies that tells the
tale. Two boys are born and brought up in similar sections
in Europe. They both look out upon similar mountains. One,
an itinerant house painter, said later in life, "I hated my father and I managed my mother." He outgrew his dependent years. He became self-assertive, and he never outgrew
that. He let it become a hard shell, shutting out any sounds
of humanity and love. Out of that twisted life came a blight
on the world, for that man's name was Adolf Hitler.

The other boy developed in the spirit of kindness and
faith. He came to think of life with reverence, and some of
the "deep calling unto deep" that went on all the time in his
life led him to believe, as he put it, "to live is to owe." His
was a growing vision of service and in that vision was the
ever growing figure of the Christ. This man, whose name is
Albert Schweitzer, wrote "He comes to us as one unknown,
as He came to the disciples by the lake shore. He speaks the
old words 'Follow me' and sets us to tasks that He would
have fulfilled in our time. He commands, and to those who
obey in the conflict and the toil and the sufferings of a living
fellowship He reveals Himself as an ineffable mystery, and
in the struggle of life they shall discover for themselves who
He is."

Such a man hears the song of eternity, "the Kingdoms of
this world are become the Kingdoms of our Lord." This man
responds in affirmation, "and He shall reign forever and
ever." His heart and mind have been opened wide to the
energy and purpose of the Lord. Though he is a subject in
the Kingdom, he faces every peril in life with courage and
calm, for he is a *nobleman in the service of The King*.

In closing this book, will you join with me in a simple
prayer, which has often been mine in the writing?

May the words of our mouths, the meditations of our hearts, the intentions of our minds, and the aspirations of our souls be acceptable unto Thee.

Almighty God, give us an ever-growing concept of our task and our destiny. As our spirit rises on the wings of reason and faith, widen our awareness till we see Thy far horizons and majestic vistas.

We acknowledge that we will not masters be until we Master find. We bow to touch the hem of Thy sovereignty. Accept our service in that Everlasting Kingdom whose banners are righteousness, justice, peace and joy, through Jesus Christ our Lord. Amen.